Sustainable Finance

Sustainable Finance is a concise and authoritative reference series linking research and practice. It provides reliable concepts and research findings in the ever growing field of sustainable investing and finance, SDG economics and Leadership with the declared commitment to present the theories, methods, tools and investment approaches that can fulfil the United Nations Sustainable Development Goals and the Paris Agreement COP 21/22 alongside with de-risking assets and creating triple purpose solutions that ensure the parity of profit, people and planet through choice architecture passion and performance. The series addresses market failure, systemic risk and reinvents portfolio theory, portfolio engineering as well as behavioural finance, financial mediation, product innovation, shared values, community building, business strategy and innovation, exponential tech and creation of social capital. Sustainable Finance and SDG Economics series helps to understand keynotes on international guidelines, guiding accounting and accountability principles, prototyping new developments in triple bottom line investing, cost benefit analysis, integrated financial first plus impact first concepts and impact measurement. Going beyond adjacent fields (like accounting, marketing, strategy, risk management) it integrates the concept of psychology, innovation, exponential tech, choice architecture, alternative economics, blue economy shared values, professions of the future, leadership, human and community development, team culture, impact, quantitative and qualitative measurement, Harvard Negotiation, mediation and complementary currency design using exponential tech and ledger technology. Books in the series contain latest findings from research, concepts for implementation, as well as best practices and case studies for the finance industry.

Harald J. Bolsinger • Johannes Hoffmann •
Bernd Villhauer
Editors

The European Central Bank and Its Role in a Sustainable Finance System

Springer

Editors
Harald J. Bolsinger
Technical University of Applied Sciences
Würzburg-Schweinfurt (THWS)
Würzburg, Germany

Johannes Hoffmann
Goethe University Frankfurt
Frankfurt, Germany

Bernd Villhauer
Weltethos-Institut
Tübingen, Baden-Württemberg, Germany

ISSN 2522-8285 ISSN 2522-8293 (electronic)
Sustainable Finance
ISBN 978-3-031-24477-3 ISBN 978-3-031-24478-0 (eBook)
https://doi.org/10.1007/978-3-031-24478-0

This Springer imprint is published by the registered company Springer Nature Switzerland AG
The registered company address is: Gewerbestrasse 11, 6330 Cham, Switzerland

Foreword

Ladies and Gentlemen,

It gives me great pleasure to welcome you today to the Goethe University.

First of all, I would like to thank the organizers of today' s conference, and especially Dr. Villhauer and Professor Hoffmann, and to welcome those who will be presenting papers to the conference.

I would also like to welcome the members of the Research Group on Finance and Business and all other colleagues present.

In the past, theology used to be oriented solely towards the next world and concerned itself exclusively with the message of the Gospels and with revelation. Those days have long passed. The Goethe University has traditionally been closely involved in this shift of emphasis, and I would like to pay tribute here to our research project Theologie Interkulturell, or Intercultural Theology, as an example.

Now that humanity has become "our second skin" in the electronic age, to quote the Canadian philosopher Marshall McLuhan, much has changed since we have become aware of this. This is particularly noticeable where young people are concerned, and here at the Goethe University it is visible in the activities of the Green Office, which is organized by the students; theological scholarship is changing too and is broadening its object of investigation.

The Frankfurter Forschungsgruppe Ethisch-Ökologisches Rating, or Research Group on Ethical-Ecological Rating, which was founded by the (late) economist Gerhard Scherhorn together with the moral theologian Johannes Hoffmann, who is present today, has been considering many of the recent changes within the field. Right from the start, the structure of the research methods employed by the group was interdisciplinary, transdisciplinary, intercultural, and ecumenical. Female and male scholars, students, and, if I may put it this way, practitioners with many years of professional experience work together in the research group. And furthermore, the word "rating" expresses an aspiration that is the research group's own: the findings should no longer be pure theory, but should be of practical use.

The goal is to identify values and norms that can be used to shape the world. Does this mean that the world should be made in the image of the findings of academic research? A world shaped by knowledge that comes into existence via an open dialogue, after the weighing up of all aspects and relevant factors and through our awareness of human responsibility for the Anthropocene? This is a target-oriented idea, one that carries a heavy burden of responsibility for the president of a university where knowledge for sustainability, justice, and the development of society in the twenty-first century is being elaborated!

Ladies and gentlemen, the basic requirements for this are twofold: on the one hand, the trust placed by society in scientific findings, which is very valuable and must constantly be earned anew by means of transparency and reflection on scientific methods, and, on the other hand, being prepared and actively striving to transfer these findings to the space where political decisions are made and to society.

We are responsible ourselves for the first of these and receive support for our efforts to transfer knowledge. For example, a Federal Agency for Disruptive Innovation has been set up and magic words like "start-ups" and "social entrepreneurship" are omnipresent. And when one sees what can happen when something new is also urgently needed (one only needs to think of a certain vaccine which, in just over a year, was researched, tested, manufactured, and made commercially available) one can appreciate that this may be a good way of proceeding: those of us working in universities, especially, are not only researchers but also teachers, and the concept and scope of teaching need to be understood in a broad sense. We want to pass our knowledge on.

While I was preparing these welcoming remarks for today's conference, it struck me that the Research Group is engaged in connecting theology and the world of finance by means of the hinge of sustainability and that this generates a shared approach or level of analysis. It makes it possible, in accordance with what is expected of science today, to examine a question from different perspectives and using the tools of the widest range of disciplines, and in this way to grasp the full complexity of problems arising in a globalized world.

Thinking problems together, thinking globally, is a challenge. If one pursues a certain question or a certain interest together with others, those involved need to develop a shared language, an overarching understanding of the complexities, if they are to be able to take everything into account when formulating hypotheses—and so to live up to the demands of a science that reflects on its own methods.

Ladies and gentlemen, this process can be painful. Knowledge produced by individual disciplines can, will, and must be placed in question in the light of transdisciplinarity. No single discipline enjoys sovereignty in joint work, and added value only comes into being when one turns towards a new transdisciplinary way of thinking and accepts that new disciplines with future-oriented ambitions of their own will emerge out of transdisciplinarity.

This is precisely what the Research Group wants, and it wants more than that: it wants to discuss these issues with practitioners and to cooperate with them—in other words, to go even further in thinking the idea of transdisciplinarity. All sides, not just science but also the perspectives of society, the economy, and politics, should be involved.

In my view this is the right course to follow. We as scientists, and especially we as members of a university with its unique distinguishing features, want to create sustainability. And, yes, we want to transfer it to society.

Moreover, with this goal of developing knowledge for societal development, sustainability, and justice in the twenty-first century we are also, as scientists and as the Goethe University, increasingly acting politically. We can no longer hide behind the claim that our assumptions are purely theoretical and that we are politically objective. As society changes we change too, but we promise that we will not leave the sphere of science and that we understand our findings as something we offer to others.

The Research Group on Ethical-Ecological Rating has also changed. It is now headed by Dr. Bernd Villhauer, who is General Manager of the Weltethos-Institut or Global Ethics Institute at the University of Tübingen. It also has a new name and is now called the Research Group on Finance and Business. Did the ethics of ecological rating get lost on the way to Baden-Württemberg? By no means. On the Group's website, and elsewhere too I am sure, Dr. Villhauer writes: "An ethically based and sustainability-oriented financial system is not only possible, it is also urgently needed."

Another thing that has not changed is the striving of the Research Group to exert an influence on the general process of developing an informed opinion. As I understand it, the Group were pioneers in this field in the 1990s: the project of working out an ethical-ecological rating on the basis of scientific criteria. The fact that they are continuing this work, in a different form of course, is something that should be celebrated.

Ladies and gentlemen, the process of creating knowledge, whether in the political sphere or in writing the latest standard work in an academic field, always involves the temptation to convince other people. And it is true that one can sometimes lose one's temper as one tries to do so. But debate, and especially debating with those who do not share one's position, is constitutive: and where can such conversations take place, if not in the university? For this reason, I would also like to make a special point here of thanking our colleagues from the world of practice who have accepted the challenge of an open discussion in an academic environment. It is not self-evident that this should happen, but it is extremely important, for it is in such discussions that academic findings can be refined and the transfer of knowledge tested.

Once again, I would like to welcome you all to the Goethe University; for all our sakes, I hope you will enjoy a productive conference.

Johann Wolfgang Goethe University Frankfurt
Frankfurt am Main, Germany

Enrico Schleiff

Contents

About the Editors

Harald J. Bolsinger is the former Dean and Vice-Dean of the Faculty of Economics and Business Administration at the Technical University of Applied Sciences Würzburg-Schweinfurt (THWS), Germany. He gained extensive practical experience in corporate customer care and sales in the cooperative banking sector, as an economic promoter for the city of Nuremberg, Germany, and in independent management consultancy. He is active in numerous initiatives to promote sustainable corporate governance, corporate responsibility, and Christian values in business and academic life. He has taught at various universities, and his current focus is chiefly on sustainable corporate management and values management, as well as business ethics issues. He served in the Research Group Finance and Economy of the Weltethos Institute at the University of Tübingen as Director Regulatory Policy (Member of the Board) until January 2023.

Johannes Hofmann was in charge of developing the Frankfurt-Hohenheimer catalogue, providing the most comprehensive criteria for ethical investments with over 800 evaluation criteria the basis for assigning sustainability ratings to many companies worldwide. He is Chairman of the Founding Board of the Research Group Finance and Economy of the Weltethos Institute at the University of Tübingen.

Bernd Villhauer is Managing Director of the Global Ethic Institute (WEIT) at the University of Tübingen, Germany and has taught at the universities of Karlsruhe, Jena, Darmstadt, and Tübingen. His main research interests are in cultural and media science issues, as well as theoretical and practical philosophy and economics. He is the co-founder of the Institute for Philosophy of Practice in Darmstadt, Germany and Director of the Good Governance Lab at the European School of Governance (EUSG). In the Research Group Finance and Economy of the Weltethos Institute at the University of Tübingen, he is Member of the Board (Director Research Organization).

From "Climate Finance" to "Climate Finance Society" to a Culture of Sustainability: Changing Perspectives on the ECB's New Strategy

Harald J. Bolsinger and Ulrich Klüh

Abstract In this text, all contributions are summarized and the focus of the volume is explained. It highlights the importance of a new cultural setting for ECB sustainability strategies. From a system in which the financial sector incorporates sustainability according to its own logic, as does the real sector, the political sector, the regulatory sector, and the civil society, we need to start working on a system of mutually consistent logics to move from "(ECB) Climate Finance" to a "Climate Finance Society" and from "Sustainable Finance" to a "Sustainable Finance Society." On this basis, one could then start working on the even more ambitious project of putting culture center stage.

In 2021, the European Central Bank (ECB) has finally set sail to become a serious actor in the transformation to a sustainable economy and society. After years of incremental change, it has integrated concerns about climate change in its strategy. With this focus on climate (and the associated disregard with respect to other dimensions of sustainability), the ECB mirrors developments on the level of the European Union (EU) in general. There, initiatives such as the Green Deal, the Fit for 55 program, or the EU taxonomy can be considered serious attempts to get down to business with respect to the ecological threats resulting from climate change. In contrast to the ECB, these programs make reference to other aspects of sustainable development, ranging from planetary boundaries in general to social aspects, human

Ulrich Klüh acknowledges financial support by the Federal Ministry of Education and Research of Germany in the framework of its funding initiative Sustainable Finance and Climate Protection (SFCP).

H. J. Bolsinger (✉)
Technical University of Applied Sciences Würzburg-Schweinfurt (THWS), Würzburg, Germany
e-mail: harald.bolsinger@thws.de

U. Klüh
Center for Sustainable Economic and Corporate Policy, Darmstadt, Germany
e-mail: ulrich.klueh@h-da.de

H. J. Bolsinger et al. (eds.), *The European Central Bank and Its Role in a Sustainable Finance System*, Sustainable Finance, https://doi.org/10.1007/978-3-031-24478-0_1

rights, and working conditions. Similar to the ECB, however, the EU commission's proposals are clearly biased toward the issue of climate change. And similar to the ECB, the commission acts from a deep conviction that climate change is a challenge that can be addressed within the logic of the current economic system.

The ECB's strategy on climate can be seen as a commitment to incorporate climate change considerations into its operational framework. The details of implementing this commitment are not known yet, as they will be developed under the framework of an "action plan" and "roadmap," emphasizing

- Macroeconomic modeling and assessment of implications for monetary policy transmission
- Statistical data for climate change risk analyses
- Disclosures as a requirement for eligibility as collateral and asset purchases
- Enhancement of risk assessment capabilities
- Collateral framework
- Corporate sector asset purchases

Especially the mentioning of the disclosure requirements, the collateral framework, and corporate asset purchases has led the financial community to believe that the ECB is willing to take the gloves off when it comes to climate change. However, it is still unclear how bold changes to the current rules will be. What is clear is how the ECB legitimizes its engagement in the fight against climate change. Climate change will not be considered as a stand-alone ("secondary") objective. It is introduced through its potential relevance for price stability. Its incorporation is mainly justified by the concern that "climate change and the transition towards a more sustainable economy affect the outlook for price stability" and that "climate change and the carbon transition affect the value and the risk profile of the assets held on the Eurosystem's balance sheet, potentially leading to an undesirable accumulation of climate-related financial risks" (ECB 2021a, b).

While the mentioned changes are a step forward, the new strategy has been the object of controversial discussions. Some observers, especially in Germany, fear that the ECB is taking on too much responsibility in areas not directly related to its primary mandate. Others criticize the lack of detail, concrete action, and the fact that the priorities of monetary policy remain unchanged. Others still find the ECB's reaction to be too much focused on a single sustainability issue, climate change, ignoring the fact that the challenge of planetary boundaries can only be addressed in a holistic way, taking into account the complex interplay between different boundaries and more generally the complexity of ecosystems, especially in a situation where the latter have already been severely damaged. A final group of critics emphasize the need to go beyond ecological concerns, as the transformation lying ahead of us will require a more fundamental overhaul of the way social, cultural, and ethical issues are incorporated in our ways of organizing economic activity.

In spite of the varied nature of the criticism, the academic debate on the ECB's role in the sustainability transformation has been rather one-dimensional. It has mainly focused on one perspective, mainstream economic reasoning. Within the economic sphere, it has largely relied on standard descriptions of the macro-financial nexus, such as the one associated with the so-called neoclassical synthesis. It has been highly Eurocentric, neglecting the perspectives of the Global South and what is now often called the emergence of a "terrestrial" political economy and political ecology (Latour 2018). Finally, it has been very technocratic. In its better moments, it has taken on board aspects from the political sciences, but social and cultural perspectives have been largely neglected.

On October 13, 2021, the *Research Group Finance and Economics of the Global Ethics Institute* organized a conference at Goethe University in Frankfurt/Main to "change perspectives" and in this way widen and deepen the debate on ECB sustainability. Its objective was to offer a platform for a more systematic, holistic, and multidimensional treatment of the ECB's new strategy and to organize an unremitting change

- From purely economized and modernistic to transdisciplinary and transformative perspectives, taking into account the question of how to embed the economy into the wider context of a world society under severe ecological threat
- From mainly Eurocentric to global perspectives, taking into account the importance of views from the Global South and the emergence of terrestrial perspectives
- From the economic perspectives derived from the neoclassical synthesis and mainstream finance to a more pluralistic economics, giving voice to approaches such as the Modern Monetary Theory (MMT) or economic history
- From largely technocratic to more holistic perspectives, taking on board the views from civil society, business community, sustainability research, and transformational science, and a more broader view of the limits of the economy and its specific rationality

In his welcome address to the conference, the president of the Goethe University, Enrico Schleiff, commended this intention and related it to the tradition of his university and the history of the Research Group Finance and Economics of the Global Ethic Institute. He made visible how its predecessor, the "Research Group on Ethical-Ecological Rating" (Frankfurter Forschungsgruppe Ethisch-Ökologisches Rating), had always diverged from one-dimensional approaches to finance and money and how it has continuously multiplied and integrated different perspectives. Founded by economist Gerhard Scherhorn together with moral theologian Johannes Hoffmann, it bridged theology, philosophy, and the world of finance and economy by means of the hinge of sustainability. In this way, it generated a unique shared approach and a holistic level of analysis that is upheld by its successor group at Weltethos Institute in events such as the one on the ECB.

The chairman of the founding board of the research group Johannes Hoffmann gave an overview of the sustainability situation in the global financial markets directly after Schleiff's thematic introduction: "Sustainable Finance: What Has Happened—What Needs to Happen?" He made clear how much has changed already and how sustainability has become a mainstream concern. He also emphasized, however, that much of the current thinking in the area of sustainable finance is characterized by a tendency to preserve the existing logics of finance and by a lack to take into account ethical and cultural dimensions more systematically.

Afterward, Peter Ehrlich, representing the ECB, presented the new climate strategy in his contribution "The Role of the ECB in the Climate Crisis." He emphasized the need for much more analytical work and the fact that a meaningful agreement has been reached in spite of different views on the role of central banks in areas other than price stability. He also made clear that the ECB's climate policy engagement has only just begun and that the role of central banks is to facilitate the politically desired transition to a carbon-neutral economy, not to become a political actor itself. Finally, he expressed his conviction that the ECB is confident to be able to combine a proactive role in climate policy with a firm commitment to its mandate, especially its primary goal of price stability.

The following discussion made it clear that this will prove to be a daunting task, especially because of the extraordinary high degree of independence of the ECB. The explicit type of coordination with other players in climate policy that is precluded by such independence might soon prove to be a sizeable burden on leveraging the potential of monetary and supervisory policies for the Green Deal. This independence, in turn, also makes it very difficult and challenging to take on board other aspects of the ongoing transformation toward a more sustainable society and to a more ethical approach to finance. Aspects such as market neutrality might continue to stand in the way of mobilizing finance for the common good.

Against this backdrop, it is not really surprising that fundamental human rights have not been integrated into the core operations of the ECB. In fact, they did not even become a serious issue during the discussions on climate policy. Harald J. Bolsinger illustrated this through his account of the experiences made with EU petition 429/2017, which tried to increase the pressure on policymakers inside and outside the ECB to incorporate at least minimum standards now expected by any player in the markets, independent of its mandate. It seems to be a long way to stop the systematic ethical blindness of the Eurosystem. This became clear in the second part of the progress report given by Harald J. Bolsinger and Jens Minnemann. The description of the political developments related to the petition raised questions about the credibility of the ECB and the EU institutions responsible for fundamental rights compliance. Up to now (06/2022), the basic problem is still not resolved.

Adding a practical view of a financial market actor, Jens Minnemann followed up on the crucial issue of credibility, a term that is much too often reserved for a central bank commitment to just one objective, price stability. Minnemann made clear that further normative aspects and attitudes need to be included before one can truly speak about the credibility of a financial intermediary. The ECB would need to rethink whether its notion of credibility could continue to be derived merely from narrow macroeconomic reasoning or would need to be interpreted more broadly. In Minnemann's contribution to the book on hand, a basic scientific classification of credibility and hands-on experiences from dealing with banks are included.

Together with Harald J. Bolsinger's chapter, Minnemann's contribution puts forward a bold hypothesis: that being credible in financial markets requires to fully respect fundamental human rights in all operations and to protect them in all aspects of business. Issues such as market neutrality or even the "primary" can then only be secondary. Instead of discussing the limits of the EU Charter of Fundamental Rights for ages, Minnemann and Bolsinger argue implicitly the ECB should just change the way it interprets the Treaties.

In the following panel discussion, moderated by Bernd Villhauer, further light was shed on the difficult strategic and moral dilemmas the ECB is facing. In the 1990s, when the Treaties were written and the ECB's mandate was set up, the Zeitgeist was that fighting inflation was the only thing a central bank should be allowed to do and that political interference was a sure way to macroeconomic disaster. Strict inflation targeting and central bank independence were sometimes even elevated to the level of ethical standards. While the dramatic consequences of climate change, biodiversity loss, and other socio-ecological problems are changing the way the public thinks about priorities, the legal framework did not. The panel provided at least four ways for the ECB to deal with this dilemma.

The first is to rely on the legal and institutional changes within the EU and to argue that they provide a way for the central bank to reinterpret its new role. A crucial role might be played by the EU taxonomy for sustainable activities, which has the potential to make "finance with an impact" a mainstream policy, but also exposes remaining weaknesses in the EU's approach to sustainable finance. In his contribution to this volume, the moderator of the panel, Bernd Villhauer, takes up ideas from the discussion and highlights the key points on the need for a unified understanding of sustainability for financial markets.

A second option would be to acknowledge that lawmakers always have the right to change their mind. Ulrich Klüh and Janina Urban show that central banks have always changed in accordance with large socioeconomic transformations and that these changes have often involved a rather strong political influence. In contrast to mainstream thinking, democratic control of central banking has not always led to disaster. In contrast, history might offer the surprising conclusion that only a democratically embedded central bank might offer stability and contribute to development, at least in the long run. In a variation of Keynes, they then argue that "in the long run, we will already be swept away by climate change," so waiting for the political will to change EU Treaties is no option. Therefore, they argue for a different strategy. The language of the Treaties offers enough scope for arguing that the interpretations of the legal language put forward in the neoliberal 1990s are likely to lead to wrong policies in the transformative 2020s. For example, the language in the Treaties does not preclude explicitly in any way a parliamentary reinterpretation of the objectives the ECB should follow.

A fourth and final option put forward during the panel would be to strongly rely on fiscal measures, which are by nature closer to what is democratically controlled. This, however, would require to focus less on fiscal restraints. In the view of Modern Monetary Theory (MMT), this requires a new understanding of the way the money and financial markets work and how they are related to fiscal policy. On the panel, the MMT position was represented by Dirk Ehnts. His focus was on the question of what debt policies will be necessary for the sustainability transformation. With a plea to think supply and demand together as the strain on the planet's resources, he shows in his contribution that we need new theories that allow us to focus on the problems of present days.

The following sections present selected contributions to this conference, along with research from members of the Research Group on the ECB's role in supporting the transition to a more sustainable economy. Overall, we draw a mixed conclusion of the conference and its proceedings: The discussions about the ECB's mandate will and have to continue, and it is central that a broad public is part in discussing the basic questions of monetary and financial policy in connection with environmental, sustainability, and fundamental rights issues. The conference and this publication can only be a start. That is why the *Research Group Finance and Economics of the Global Ethics Institute* will continue to actively advocate for an ecologically, socially, and culturally compatible financial system and critically accompany developments in international financial policy.

To make climate finance and sustainable finance work, the challenge will be to overcome the different institutional logics characterizing the different segments of our society. From a system in which the financial sector incorporates sustainability according to its own logic, as does the real sector, the political sector, the regulatory sector, and the civil society, we need to start working on a system of mutually consistent logics to move from "(ECB) Climate Finance" to a "Climate Finance Society" and from "Sustainable Finance" to a "Sustainable Finance Society." On this basis, one could then start working on the even more ambitious project of putting culture center stage.

References

ECB (2021a) The ECB's monetary policy strategy statement. https://www.ecb.europa.eu/home/search/review/html/ecb.strategyreview_monpol_strategy_statement.en.html (last checked: Dec 31, 2022)

ECB (2021b) An overview of the ECB's monetary policy strategy. https://www.ecb.europa.eu/home/search/review/html/ecb.strategyreview_monpol_strategy_overview.en.html (last checked: Dec 31, 2022)

Latour B (2018) Das terrestrische Manifest, translated by Bernd Schwibs, Berlin: Suhrkamp

Sustainable Finance: What Has Happened—What Needs to Happen?

von Johannes Hoffmann

Abstract Looking back at the history and development of the research group, Prof. Hoffmann explains what progress has been made in implementing sustainability awareness in the financial industry as well as the political structures. The Frankfurt-Hohenheim Guidelines (FHL) played an important part in changing the way of thinking about investment, but it must be reconsidered and updated in the light of the current crises.

1 I Will Start with an Anecdote

In 1965, an Evangelical Catholic Student Day was held for all universities, for which I was responsible as the education officer of the German Catholic Student Association (KDSE) together with Jochen R. Klicker who is responsible for the Protestant Church's Student Association (ESGiD).

The preparatory commission had proposed as a theme:

"We live off the specialists, but we die from their monologues."

We had invited Prof. Dr. Max-Paul Engelmeier, professor for Neuropsychiatry at the University of Münster, to be the keynote speaker.

Engelmeier asked: "What does that mean, living off the specialists?" Among other things, he referred to the 1963 conference on the "Future of Man" organized by the CIBA Foundation and concluded: "In this respect, then, the thesis 'We live off the specialists' would be justified depressingly enough."

Involuntarily, specialist Mario Draghi came to my mind, who claimed for himself and the ECB that in his work as a specialist he was exclusively responsible for securing monetary stability in the euro area and that he had to act independently of the fundamental values of the EU Parliament.

von Johannes Hoffmann (✉)
Goethe University Frankfurt, Frankfurt, Germany
e-mail: j.hoffmann@em.uni-frankfurt.de

H. J. Bolsinger et al. (eds.), *The European Central Bank and Its Role in a Sustainable Finance System*, Sustainable Finance, https://doi.org/10.1007/978-3-031-24478-0_2

As the ECB is an institution of the EU Parliament, we dispute this view of Draghi and will try to justify this in today's meeting. We maintain that the ECB, when issuing government and corporate bonds, must also keep in mind the development of the climate and sustainability for the survival of the world and its people. The ECB cannot leave this concern to others alone, to the banks, the companies, and the financial service providers.

There have been great successes in the last 20 years. However, the volumes that the ECB has to deal with are much more effective in achieving the sustainability goals that the EU and the United Nations have decided on.

2 What Has Happened in the Financial Industry So Far?

Everyone can observe that "ethical investment" has left its niche existence and became mainstream. As a prerequisite for this, numerous sustainability agencies have developed production sustainability assessments of companies and capital investments in a very differentiated manner.

The Frankfurt-Hohenheim Guidelines (FHL), for example, were developed at this university. At the beginning of the 1990s, the research group Ethical-Ecological Rating developed together with then oekom research AG a scientific criterion as a fundament and implemented it in a rating concept. This rating was adopted and used by the ISS (Institutional Shareholder Services) in New York in 2018 to evaluate capital investments. This year, the Frankfurt Stock Exchange bought it with a major stake. So, you could say, the FHL came back to Frankfurt.

Despite all the progress made by the ESG investment industry, time and again, it is criticized. Timo Busch, Alexander Bassen, and Kerstin Lopatta have taken a thorough look at the pros and cons in the Handelsblatt Business Briefing. They come to the conclusion: "The ESG investment industry is on the right path."

3 What Needs to Happen?

As we all know, all sustainability ratings are based on "best-in-class ratings" even when using exclusion criteria. This does create ethical competition for more sustainability in companies and financial investments. However, this is no longer sufficient in today's situation: we must achieve that the egoism of entrepreneurs, shareholders, and managers is limited, that, for example, companies cannot pass on costs to the ecological, social, and cultural common good. In this way, companies and shareholders have constantly made a lot of profits at the expense of the ecological, social, and cultural common good. The incredible volumes on the financial markets are telling evidence of this. This must end now, and companies and shareholders must be obliged to pay back to the common good in the course of the transformation to climate-friendly production processes. In order for everyone to understand this, we need legal regulations. We should demand that the new government, which has all committed themselves to protecting the climate in their election manifestos, creates these laws. This would be a very effective protection for the preservation of our climate and biodiversity.

Thus, the further development of the understanding of sustainability must open up self-control, but also social control, for companies about what and how much they are obliged to contribute to the preservation and cultivation of the natural, social/cultural, and real economic foundations of life and production. Japan has shown us how companies can do this with its Top Runner Approach to climate protection.

The Top Runner Approach was enacted by the Japanese Ministry of Economy (METI) before the United Nations Kyoto Conference as part of an amendment to an energy conservation law to show the world that it is possible to do things differently and also to do excellent business worldwide. At first, the Energy Conservation Act did not meet with the approval of industry. In the meantime, the opposite has happened. For the Top Runner, it not only proved to be an excellent instrument for reducing greenhouse gas emissions but also ensured a reduction in production costs and contributed to the development of innovations to improve energy efficiency. Both the reduction of production costs through energy efficiency and, in addition, the innovations developed to increase energy efficiency provided competitive advantages on the world market.

How does the Top Runner model work? The Toprunner approach appoints the most energy-efficient average of a manufacturer's sold products within a product group at the time of the base year as the 'Toprunner'. All other manufacturers of products in this product group must have achieved the prescribed efficiency value by a certain target year. A product category is subdivided into different product groups to account for different sizes, weight classes or even special devices of the individual products. The target year was set according to the average technical life cycle of the products in the respective product categories. However, this calculation assumes constant sales figures between base and target year.

The approach also provides for a sanction mechanism. If a manufacturer fails to achieve the top runner value of the respective product group by the target year, METI first sends a reminder. Further non-compliance is followed by publication of the manufacturer's name and an order to implement efficiency improvement measures. If this is also not followed, there is the threat of a fine and finally ban on offering the product on the Japanese market." A very simple symbolism is used to indicate to consumers whether a product, e.g., a passenger car, meets or does not meet the requirements or whether the product scores above average in energy efficiency. The Top Runner model achieves two effects:

1. Transparency in purchasing is ensured, which is easily recognizable for the consumer in this way.
2. Externalization of costs to environmental, social, and cultural commons is reduced.

Moreover, sustainability on this legal basis would be a comprehensive and fundamental economic concept. Gerhard Scherhorn, who led the research group

Ethical Ecological Rating with me for 20 years, has described such a breakthrough for comprehensive sustainability in the economy, finance, and society as an alternative to capitalism. I agree with this.

Our conference delegates of the Club of Rome have pointed out the urgency of a holistic sustainability transformation and the role of the ECB from a global perspective. A market economy in which the externalization of environmental, social, and cultural costs is prohibited by law is the alternative to neoliberalism necessary for the life of the world and its people. And for this, we must hold our government to account. Sandrine Dixson-Decléve can point out at the climate summit in Glasgow that the Club of Rome already stated quite clearly 50 years ago in the report "The Limits to Growth": "If the increase in world population, industrialisation, pollution, food production and exploitation of natural resources continues unabated, the absolute limits to growth on earth will be reached within the next hundred years."

I am confident that in the presentations and discussions of this conference, we can reinforce the urgency of radical sustainability at all levels of action. I hope that our future government will have the courage to follow Japan's example and legislate accordingly.

The New Sustainability Strategy of the ECB

Peter Ehrlich

Abstract Fast and orderly transitions to carbon-neutral economies are possible and necessary. They are also cheaper for everyone, including banks and industry. To understand the role of the ECB in creating a sustainable financial system, we have to look at the financial activities of the ECB itself, monetary policy, communication and interaction with banks, and administrative actions on different levels. Fortunately, there are European frameworks and institutions on which the ECB activities and initiatives can be based.

1 The Role of the ECB in the Climate Crisis

Sustainability is understood broadly in the financial world, very often under the term stability. For example, a sustainable financial system needs rules; it needs sustainable public finances; it needs price stability. The issue of climate or comprehensive environmental sustainability plays an important role for central banks because it can shake the pillars of a sound financial system and at the very least challenge the standard economic models, thus permanently calling financial stability into question.

Environmental sustainability, however, is still a fairly new topic for central banks. The "Network for Greening the Financial System" (NGFS) was only founded in 2017, at that time by eight central banks; by 2022, 108 central banks are already members. Incidentally, the founding chairman was Frank Elderson, who has been on the ECB Executive Board since the end of 2020.

The very fact that central banks are addressing the climate issue at all is politically controversial. Perhaps somewhat less frequently than a year or two ago, there are still comments from experts and journalists who think we are exceeding our mandate by doing so. On the other side, there are civil society organizations that think the ECB is not doing enough or is even supporting activities that are harmful to the climate.

P. Ehrlich (✉)
European Central Bank, Frankfurt, Germany
e-mail: peter.ehrlich@ecb.europa.eu

H. J. Bolsinger et al. (eds.), *The European Central Bank and Its Role in a Sustainable Finance System*, Sustainable Finance, https://doi.org/10.1007/978-3-031-24478-0_3

That's why it was important that the Governing Council unanimously adopted a climate action plan as part of its comprehensive strategic review concluded in July 2021. ECB President Christine Lagarde was a driving force behind this.

For the ECB, the issue of climate and sustainability plays an important role in three areas:

1. In its core area, monetary policy
2. In banking supervision
3. In its day-to-day work, from building management to missions and in its own facilities outside monetary policy

2 Monetary Policy

Monetary policy is the primary task of any central bank. The ECB has a singular primary mandate: to maintain price stability. The precise definition of price stability is not laid down in the EU Treaties but may be defined by the Governing Council of the ECB, as confirmed by rulings of the ECJ. The definition of price stability established in the aforementioned strategic review is a medium-term inflation rate of 2%. The 2% target is the international standard, even though it was not achieved in current figures or structurally in OECD economies for many years before 2021.

The Governing Council decision of 8 July 2021 states:

> Addressing climate change is a global challenge and a policy priority for the European Union. While it is primarily the responsibility of governments and parliaments to take action on climate change, the ECB recognizes the need to integrate climate change considerations into its monetary policy framework within its mandate.

The reasons are clear: climate change and the transition to a more sustainable economy affect the outlook for price stability, as they impact macroeconomic indicators such as inflation, output, employment, interest rates, investment and productivity, financial stability, and monetary policy transmission. In addition, climate change and the transition to a low-carbon economy have implications for the value and risk profile of assets on the Eurosystem balance sheet. This could, for example, lead to an undesirable concentration of climate-related financial risks.

The direct link of our climate decisions to the primary mandate of price stability is also legally important. Although the so-called secondary mandate—the general duty to support EU policies—also obliges us to protect the climate, here it would only be one of many objectives.

In the climate plan, the ECB commits to reviewing its monetary policy framework. The ECB's Climate Change Competence Center, which was also launched in 2021—internally, the English term Climate Change Centre is used—will coordinate the relevant activities within the ECB in close cooperation with the Eurosystem, i.e., the national central banks in the eurozone such as the Bundesbank.

The Climate Change Centre is headed by Irene Heemskerk and reports directly to President Lagarde.

Specifically, it will focus on the following:

Macroeconomic models: The ECB will accelerate the development of new macroeconomic models and conduct theoretical and empirical analyses to monitor the impact of climate change and related policies on the economy, the financial system, and monetary policy transmission through financial markets and the banking system to firms and households. Right now, after all, there is a lively public debate about the impact of climate change measures on inflation. Higher CO_2 prices increase the inflation rate, and other climate protection measures also make life more expensive at first. In the long term, however, more sustainable economic activity can also mean lower inflation and fluctuations in energy prices, which are particularly severe in times of geopolitical crisis, are likely to decrease significantly with a full supply of renewables.

Statistical data for climate change risk analysis: The ECB will develop new indicators covering relevant green financial instruments and the carbon footprint of financial institutions, as well as the climate-related physical risks to which these institutions are exposed. Starting in 2022, these indicators will be progressively developed, also in line with EU policies and initiatives on environmental sustainability disclosure and reporting.

Enhancing risk assessment capacity: The ECB will start conducting climate stress tests in 2022 to assess the Eurosystem's exposure to climate change risk. In doing so, it will use the methodology of its macroeconomic climate stress test, which was published in September 2021. In addition, the ECB will consider whether Eurosystem-approved credit rating agencies disclose information on how they incorporate climate risks into their credit ratings. Furthermore, the ECB will consider developing minimum standards for the consideration of climate risks in its internal ratings.

We have already developed a general climate stress test for this purpose, for example, to find out in which sectors and regions the risks are particularly high.

Collateral framework: The ECB will take relevant climate risks into account in the valuation and risk control of assets provided by counterparties as collateral for Eurosystem credit operations. This will ensure that all relevant risks are taken into account, including those arising from climate change.

Purchases of corporate sector securities: The ECB has already started to take relevant climate risks into account in its due diligence reviews for its purchases of corporate sector securities in its monetary policy portfolios. In the future, the ECB will add climate criteria to the rules that guide its corporate bond purchases, in line with its mandate. These criteria will include ensuring that issuers are, at a minimum, in compliance with or committed to EU legislation implementing the goals of the Paris Agreement.

In addition, by the first quarter of 2023, the ECB will begin publishing climate-related information on the Corporate Sector Purchase Programme (CSPP). This will also play a role when net bond purchases are discontinued, as maturing bonds are first replaced by other bonds.

In all of this, there is a close link to EU measures and initiatives in the area of disclosure and reporting on environmental sustainability. These include the

Corporate Sustainability Reporting Directive, the Taxonomy Regulation, and the Regulation on sustainability-related disclosure requirements in the financial services sector.

As part of its public sector bond purchases, the ECB already has many sustainable bonds in its portfolio, roughly estimated at about 20% of its holdings.

3 Banks

The second major area to come is banking supervision. Since 2014, the ECB has directly supervised the 100 or so largest banks in the eurozone and coordinates the supervision of all banks.

As early as last November 2021, the ECB's banking supervision published guidelines on how to deal with climate and environmental risks. Because, unlike central banks, banks finance the real economy directly and on behalf of their customers—ultimately from coal-fired power plants to sustainable food startups—we have told all banks that we expect them to develop a comprehensive and forward-looking strategy that identifies the risks and describes how to deal with risks from global warming, from loss of biodiversity, or from pollution.

First of all, the banks are doing self-assessments. We will compare these and then discuss them with the institutions as part of our supervisory dialogs. Banks do not yet have a real overview of their climate risks. That is why the ECB called on the banking sector to step up its efforts in March 2022, because banks' risk management has not yet met the requirements and 90% of banks have either only partially aligned their risk management with the ECB's requirements or not at all.

The assessment of climate risks will gradually be integrated into the annual supervisory process and thus ultimately also influence the capital requirements for banks. In the 2022 bank stress test, the focus will be on climate stress. So risk disclosure is the first step, and integration into risk-weighted capital requirements is the next step that may follow in our country and internationally.

All our analyses show a fast and orderly transition to a carbon-neutral economy is cheaper for everyone, including banks and industry, than a hot house scenario or an abrupt brake on emissions.

4 Administrative Action and Our Own Financial Investment

As an EU institution, we must of course comply with the legal requirements and should even be a pioneer. This plays a role in building management, for example; fortunately, our main building has already been designed to be low-energy and certified accordingly. Even though there will be more physical meetings in Frankfurt again after the end of the pandemic restrictions, the Governing Council has decided that the numerous committees should hold less than 50% of their meetings physically in the future. A few years ago, the ECB used to send out printed brochures and studies; that has been completely discontinued. The ECB's pension fund has committed to investments in line with ESG criteria, and this is also the approach taken by national central banks, some of which have traditionally had large assets.

5 Summary

The ECB's climate policy commitment has only just begun. The man-made climate crisis will have a major impact on our work, as it will on that of many other institutions. In Europe, this is happening within a legal framework and institutions—something that is still lacking at the international level. The role of central banks is to facilitate the politically desired transition to a carbon-neutral economy.

Independently Green? An Integrated Strategy for a Transformative ECB

Ulrich Klüh and Janina Urban

Abstract What should be the role of the ECB in tackling the socio-ecological challenges related to planetary boundaries, such as climate change and loss of biodiversity? A clear answer to this question is still lacking, in spite of the strategy review of 2021. Regretfully, this review has not received the scrutiny it deserves, as the pandemic and the war in Ukraine have taken center stage. Taking these recent developments into account, we provide a critique of the new strategy. We argue that it lacks transformativity, as it subsumes climate change under the policy objective of price stability, assumes that transformations can be mastered within the structures of the past, and refrains from questioning the current institutional set-up. In its main part, the paper discusses the historical relevance of what we believe is the main reason for these deficits: The fear that taking up the real issues (such as independence and accountability) would make the ECB a political football in times of rising inflation. Taking these fears seriously, we show that the institutionalization of central banking has *always* reflected the transformative dynamics of their time. Consequently, if planetary boundaries represent a transformative challenge, they will radically change the ECB, too. Moreover, we provide evidence that central banks' historical transformations have *always* reflected their peculiar position as mediators between the financial and the political realm. We argue that, at the current juncture, transforming central banking implies moving away from finance and toward politics. This involves risks. However, we argue that the historical experience offers few reasons to fear a closer integration of central banking into the public sphere, *as long as the latter is dominated by democratic politics*. Consequently, if one comes to the conclusion that the ECB's current corset is too narrow, it can and should be augmented. While we do not offer a blueprint for such augmentation, we conclude

---

U. Klüh (✉)
ZNWU/SECP and Darmstadt Business School, Darmstadt, Germany
e-mail: ulrich.klueh@h-da.de

J. Urban
University Witten/Herdecke, Witten, Germany
e-mail: janina.urban@uni-wh.de

H. J. Bolsinger et al. (eds.), *The European Central Bank and Its Role in a Sustainable Finance System*, Sustainable Finance, https://doi.org/10.1007/978-3-031-24478-0_4

our analysis by sketching elements of a sustainable strategy for a transformative ECB.

1 Introduction

As the COVID-19 pandemic and the war in Ukraine have taken center stage, questions about the sustainability of the ECB and its role as an agent of socio-ecological transformation have taken a back seat. That does not make them less relevant: What should be the ECB's role in Europe's fight against climate change, biodiversity loss, and other ecological problems? How should it take into account the distributional implications of a socio-ecological transformation of the economy? Should ECB policies be integrated into the Green Deal and the Green Deal into the ECB's revised strategy? What would this imply for the institutionalization of central banking in Europe? Should a central bank, similar to other private and public financial institutions such as promotional and development banks, set itself the target to become a transformative or developmental agent, anyway?

Even though these issues have been hotly debated, they have not been resolved. The new strategy that the ECB has published in the summer of 2021 (see ECB 2021a) was an attempt to address them. But did it answer them? Or at least provide a robust framework for future analysis, for example, through the ECB's new climate change center? Regretfully, the strategy review has not received the scrutiny it deserves, so its adequacy remains contested. This is partly a result of the pandemic and the war in Ukraine.[1] Both developments have absorbed much of the attention and energy of professional observers. We believe this is highly unfortunate, as recent macroeconomic developments combine with sustainability challenges in a way that radically question the thrust of the new strategy. The geo-political risks that have materialized in Ukraine combine with the geo-ecological risks related to planetary boundaries. We might face a "new age of inflation," characterized by "climateflation, fossilflation and greenflation" (Schnabel 2022), that requires an instant rethinking of the ECB's strategic framework. Such a rethinking is necessary long before the next assessment in the context of the envisioned "regular review cycle," expected in 2025 (ECB 2021a).

Against this backdrop, the starting point of this paper is a critical look at the ECB's new strategy (Sect. 2). We show that the new framework is a step forward in

[1]The pandemic has also left its mark on the review process itself. It has distracted central banks' attention away from mostly everything but the fight against it. The ECB's strategic review process fell victim to this development. From a procedural point of view, it is disappointing to see that there has not been much of a public, academic, and political discourse. Instead of heated debates on the appropriate definition of price stability, the need to take into account a broader set of concrete secondary objectives or the dramatic challenge of climate change, we have seen rather shallow and prissy discussions. From a substantive point of view, the promise to "leave no stone unturned" (Lagarde in Canepa and Martin 2020) has been violated, for example, with respect to questions of the identification of policy goals and the cooperation with other policymakers (Angeloni 2020).

terms of policies but suffers from being rather backward-looking. It partly solves the problems the ECB had experienced since its foundation, but does not address sufficiently the challenges that can reasonably be expected. Most importantly, the new strategy fails to recognize the need to question the ECB's organizational and institutional foundations. It is devised on the view that greening the ECB can be done within the boundaries of the current set-up. By refraining from a more systemic approach that takes into account the ECB's positioning vis-à-vis other sectors and actors central to the socioeconomic transformation, it has taken a "modernist" view of the world. To become a "transformative" central bank, therefore, a broader approach is necessary, one that takes into account the need to democratically back a credible greening of central banks.

But wouldn't such a broad approach open the box of Pandora? Opponents of a more radical rethink of central banking rightly point to the risks in politicizing monetary authorities. Indeed, we believe that the main reason for the deficits of the new strategy is rooted in fears that taking up the real issues (such as independence and accountability, the role of quasi-fiscal policies in the Green Deal, and the new hierarchy of objectives that might be warranted) would make the ECB a political football in times of rising inflation. In Part 3, the paper discusses the historical relevance of these fears of "transformative" or "developmental" central banking. Taking them seriously without making them into an absolute, we show that the institutionalization of central banking has always reflected the transformative dynamics of their time. Historically, central banks are at least as much involved in supporting large-scale socioeconomic change ("development," see Epstein 2013) as they are in ensuring monetary and financial stability.

Consequently, if planetary boundaries represent a transformative challenge, it is very likely that they will radically change the ECB, too, no matter the relevance of the fears related to such change. To shape rather than incur transformative change, it is necessary to understand its nature. The analysis in Part 3 of this paper suggests that central banks' historical transformations have mainly reflected their peculiar position as mediators between the financial and the political realm. We argue that, at the current juncture, transforming central banking implies moving away from finance and toward politics. While this involves risks, the historical experience offers few reasons to fear a closer integration of central banking into the public sphere, as long as the latter is dominated by democratic politics. Consequently, if one comes to the conclusion that the ECB's current corset is too narrow, it can and should be augmented.

While we do not offer a blueprint for such augmentation, we conclude our analysis by sketching elements of a sustainable strategy for a transformative ECB (Part 4). The academic and applied discourse on greening the ECB has roughly fallen into two camps. On the one hand, there are concrete ideas on the type of policies and operations that would be consistent with a greening of the ECB (see Table 1 in the appendix). These range from revising rules for the collateral pool to a monetary financing of public investments in green infrastructures and technologies. On the other hand, we find suggestions for toughening up the ECB's institutional and organizational set-up against the backdrop of multiple goals and expectations (see Table 2 in the appendix).

While we build on some of these proposals, we believe there is a need for a more comprehensive approach, bringing these two sides of the coin together. More concretely, we see a necessity to formulate an integrated green monetary policy strategy that takes into account the multiple deliverables of the ECB as a monetary policy authority (including price and financial stability), their relationship to each other, and, most importantly, their implications for governance arrangements. In a nutshell, we argue that operational and institutional changes need to be proportional to each other: The more you want the ECB to do, the more you need to adopt governance. We therefore try to integrate the two types of proposals that have emerged recently, those on concrete policies and those on the institutionalization of a monetary policy. By doing so, we choose an approach that clearly separates itself from the idea that an independent ECB should mainly deliver on its inflation target, a position also held by some who are considered to be on the progressive side of the policy spectrum (Dullien and Tober 2021). In contrast, we set up a model of an ECB that moves from a single purpose to multiple purposes and, as a consequence, needs political guidance. We can build on a few other works in a similar spirit, in particular Couppey-Soubeyran (2020) and Couppey-Soubeyran and Delandre (2021).

In our view, such an approach would also go some way in incorporating recent developments. The pandemic and the war have severely complicated central banks' bread and butter business: keeping inflation in check while contributing to stable employment and growth. Inflation volatility has increased markedly, as commodity prices fluctuate in response to the deepest cuts in economic activity since World War II. Pundits on both sides of the Atlantic are painting a bleak picture of upcoming inflation risks. Supply bottlenecks, which had long been absent as a major concern for policymakers, are back on the agenda. This, in turn, is leading to heated debates on whether the ECB should react pro-actively when inflation creeps up or should treat inflation pressures as expression of circumstances in which sustained reflation might actually be acceptable.

The paper proceeds as follows. In Sect. 2, we critically review the new strategy, also against the backdrop of recent developments. Section 3 shows that the institutional set-up of central banks is historically contingent and that mandates, governance, and accountability arrangements have always been adopted to the specific historical context. While context is key, there are a number of constant struggles and conflicts that need to be taken into account to design robust frameworks. We argue that these struggles and conflicts are crucial when designing an institutional set-up but need not to be taken to the extreme. In our view, the ECB's current institutional set-up is such an extreme, as it embodies a very radical interpretation of central bank independence. This interpretation stands in the way of a credible and democratic greening. As a consequence, making the ECB sustainable will necessarily involve a review of objectives, instruments, and governance. In Sect. 4, we sketch policies and arrangements that could strike a better balance between operational effectiveness, speedy implementation, and democratic legitimacy. We present an integrated proposal that takes into account the current macroeconomic context, including concrete changes of policy objectives, policy measures, operations, and institutional backing. Section 5 concludes.

2 The Strategy Review: A Critical Look

Formulating the new ECB strategy has been a contentious process, with strongly opposing views. Debates have been multifaceted, but German and French views of the scope and nature of monetary policies have again been a characteristic feature, in particular with respect to the incorporation of climate change. What has been achieved is a rather fragile compromise, with two main pillars (see ECB 2021a, b).[2] The first pillar consists of a revision of the inflation targeting framework the ECB is following. Most importantly, the new target of a two (instead of less than but close to two) percent increase of the Harmonized Index of Consumer Prices (HICP) is now symmetric, implying some more leeway for letting inflation run its course. Moreover, the strategy recognizes the challenges of the effective lower bound, implying a rationale for a more elaborate set of instruments and a larger tolerance for periods in which inflation is moderately above the target.

The second pillar is a commitment to incorporate climate change considerations. The details of implementing this commitment are not known yet, as they will be developed under the framework of a work plan, emphasizing macroeconomic modeling and assessment, statistical data for climate change risk analyses, disclosures as a requirement for eligibility as collateral and asset purchases, enhancement of risk assessment capabilities, collateral framework, and corporate sector asset purchases. Some of these measures represent concrete steps to improve financing conditions for the green transformation. However, the strategy documents do not directly address the ECB's role in making sure that the transition to a sustainable economy will not founder due to inadequate finance. Rather, the language of the strategy statement hints to the fact that taking into account climate change is strictly subsumed under the primary mandate:

> Climate change has profound implications for price stability through its impact on the structure and cyclical dynamics of the economy and the financial system. Addressing climate change is a global challenge and a policy priority for the EU. Within its mandate, the Governing Council is committed to ensuring that the Eurosystem fully takes into account, in line with the EU's climate goals and objectives, the implications of climate change and the carbon transition for monetary policy and central banking. Accordingly, the Governing Council has committed to an ambitious climate-related action plan. (ECB 2021a)

Subsuming climate change under the primary mandate while mentioning concrete measures that are related to financing conditions in its action plan raises an important

[2]We abstract from elements of the new strategy that, in our view, are not either of central importance or of limited novelty. This applies, in particular, to the parts of the strategy that refer to inflation measurement, integrated assessment, communication, and periodical reassessment.

issue that the ECB does not elaborate on: What if financing conditions and inflation require different policies? Technically, the primary objective, price stability, always trumps secondary mandates, but climate change is taken on board on the back of price stability. The fact that secondary mandates are mentioned in another part of the document without any guidance with respect to their nature and prioritization adds to the confusion, rather than dissolving it.

In a similar vein, the strategy refrains from discussing concrete links between the reform of the inflation targeting framework and climate change. Though the two pillars of the strategy review are related in many ways, the relevant documents largely abstracts from these relationships. Most importantly, climate change (and the political response to it) might lead to developments in goods and asset prices that might make the increased flexibility, the ECB has given itself with respect to price stability, comes in handy. It is unclear, however, whether flexibility has increased sufficiently. Did the ECB add enough flexibility to its framework to accommodate the kind of shocks and secular developments that might be expected from a socio-economic, potentially "great" transformation? And is it enough to take these issues into account implicitly, rather than acknowledging explicitly that a socioeconomic transformation might require a different approach toward price stability?

It is beyond the scope of this paper to critically evaluate the new strategy on the basis of a complete reading of the relevant scientific literature on best practices in monetary policy strategy, inflation targeting frameworks, and the macro-financial implications of climate change (and planetary boundaries more generally). Rather, we base our assessment on a heuristic, combining three distinctions that usually define the revision of strategies: backward- versus forward-looking elements, changing policies versus institutions, and employing a mindset of modernization versus a mindset of transformation:

- Backward-looking elements emphasize what has been learned under the old strategy, while forward-looking elements ask which new challenges and circumstances can reasonably be expected. The new ECB strategy is clearly dominated by the former, with climate change being the only major forward-looking element. All other changes to monetary policy arrangements are about learning lessons from the past, and the explanatory document even speaks of departing from a "past inflation narrative" (ECB 2021b). The problem of the zero lower bound and of deflationary pressures has very much dominated ECB policies since the financial crisis of 2008. This has created pressures to adopt the inflation targeting regime and the operational frameworks to these situations, including with respect to the role of asset prices in inflation measurement.
- While new *policies* emphasize the strategies and tactics of a concrete actor, new *institutions* emphasize the rules of the game this actor is involved in. The new ECB strategy is focused on policies, but does change a number of rules and conventions. In particular, adopting a new definition of price stability and emphasizing a single policy issue such as the climate should be seen as a form of institutional change. This change, however, is limited to those institutions that the ECB can set for itself. While the ECB did reach out to "listen" to external

stakeholders, it never entered into a process in which all relevant actors (including the national European legislative and executive bodies, civil society, private and public financial market participants) would jointly discuss the arrangements of their interaction.

- Modernization is a change that is taking place within the boundaries of an organization or social system, while transformation is a change of the way in which different social systems influence and irritate each other. The former is more incremental in the sense of updating existing strategies and procedures, the latter more disruptive.[3] Based on this definition, the new strategy cannot be easily characterized as either "transformative" or "modernist." On the one hand, a "transformative" approach would have required an acknowledgment that planetary boundaries require a more general reconsideration of central bank objectives, institutions, and the interplay of the monetary authority with other actors. Such an acknowledgment is not made, at least not explicitly. On the other hand, climate change is generally considered a problem that requires transformation in the way defined above, so emphasizing it would appear as a willingness on the part of the ECB to engage with other actors to transform monetary and financial policies more radically.

From the perspective of such a three-tiered analysis, we see three main deficits with respect to the new strategy. The first deficit is related to the revision of the inflation targeting framework. While going in the right direction, it is very timid and backward-looking. It is timid because 2% is still a very low target, considering the lessons of Great Recession (see Blanchard et al. 2010), and since the new strategy does not include any "makeup" component (for a detailed discussion, see Reichlin et al. 2021). It is backward-looking because it correctly draws some of the macroeconomic lessons from the Great Recession, but does not sufficiently take into account the challenges of the fundamental transformation lying ahead of us. In particular, the strategy incorporates the experience of operating at the zero lower bound and in a lowflation environment, but not the expectation that developments in the future might be characterized by alternating spells of lowflation and higher inflation pressures. Large transformations, as the one envisioned by the Green Deal, lead to a fundamental shift and rewiring of the economy (Land 2019b) that may result in additional inflation. A smooth transition to a sustainable economy will

[3]Our definition of transformation builds on the distinction between different "futures of sustainability," as put forward by Adloff and Neckel (2019), and on the way social systems theory describes processes of modernization. Always keeping in mind Polanyi's use of the term "transformation," we envision a process that is, at least in early stages, actor-driven but, over time, develops momentum. Social systems that have functionally differentiated in a process of modernization for some time transcend their systems logic and operate in coupled modes, in a process called transition, which includes a counter-hegemonic challenge. When transition makes room for a new round of modernization, transformation has been completed. For an economist, such a transformation can be described as a switch to a new macro-regime (Klüh 2015), for example, the switch from the gold standard to the Bretton Woods regime.

require the ECB to accommodate respective pressures. As a consequence, the new framework is not sufficiently robust for the macroeconomic challenges ahead.

The second deficit, which is even more fundamental than the first one, is related to the fact that every good strategy starts with a clarification of the mission and objectives of an organization. While it had to be expected that it would not be easy for the ECB to escape the trap of the single-mindedness of its current focus on price stability, the new strategy falls strongly behind of what would have been possible within the framework provided by the Treaties. For example, it would have been feasible to clarify the way in which secondary objective factors in the ECB strategy, given that price stability is, or is expected, to be achieved over the medium term. To be able to forge a compromise with the Bundesbank, which was strongly opposed to a clarification of the fact that the ECB is indeed following multiple objectives, climate change had to be subsumed under the primary mandate. By doing so, the ECB opted for a very confusing system of objectives and targets. In the future, that will make it much more complicated to understand and communicate policies, as the statement cited above already shows.

Solving these two core issues would already go a long way in making the ECB more sustainable. By increasing the flexibility of the inflation targeting framework, the ECB would gain a substantial amount of additional room for maneuver in the uncharted waters of monetary climate policy. More clarity on the role of secondary objectives, which the ECB could provide itself, and more guidance in terms of their nature and prioritization, which would have to be provided by the Parliament and the Council, could serve as a coherent compass for the direction monetary and banking policies should take whenever the first mandate is, or is expected to be, achieved.

But there is a third problem, which is perhaps the most fundamental one (apart from issues of democratic legitimacy discussed below). A successful Green Deal will require a substantial amount of coordination between fiscal, financial, banking, and monetary policies. The eurozone has been short of sufficient coordination mechanisms between the monetary and fiscal sphere (Reichlin and Schoenmaker 2020). This lack of coordination will be felt much more strongly in the years to come, as the aftermath of the COVID-19 pandemic and the exigencies of the Green Deal create new fiscal challenges. Moreover, the Green Deal intensifies a trend that Mertens and Thiemann (2019) describe as the emergence of a new kind of European investment state. A major element of this investment state is the increasing importance of public financial institutions, in particular development and promotional banks, but also entities such as the European Stability Mechanism (ESM). To be successful as agents of a sustainability transformation, these financial (and often quasi-fiscal) entities have to be coordinated with monetary and fiscal actors. Finally, many of the ECB's options to support a quick transition to sustainability require an alignment of the regulatory policies decided in Brussels with the supervisory and monetary policies decided in Frankfurt. For example, a powerful tool to enforce better sustainability reporting and more sustainability investment is to make eligibility to the ECB's collateral pool and asset purchase programs dependent on certain disclosure requirements. The ECB could be the stick with which the EU enforces its ambitious plans for better disclosure. This, however, requires more than mere information exchange, but joint action.

Overall, the review underlines the attachment to a narrow interpretation of the European treaty and only corrects upon some consensuses built around the measurement and formulation of the inflation target. It leaves secondary goals without a clearer relation to the first one, also circling out environmental policies as a core concern. The evaluation of unconventional policies is kept to the ex post political sphere of the proportionality of decisions. Putting central bank policies in their broader political and economic environment, Reichlin et al. (2021) show why understanding and incorporating the fiscal aspects of monetary policy matter so much. The strategy review could have reacted to this growing academic consensus by providing clarity about the significance of augmented balance sheets and the risks for economic stability.

It is worth noting that the deeper reasons for these deficits do not only originate in the fissures and peculiarities of the ECB itself. Rather, there has been a lack of proactive participation of lawmakers, who should have insisted that the broad and deep type of independence, the ECB has been granted by a specific reading of the Treaties in the 1990s, needs to be reconsidered. The deficits of the new strategy show that the ECB's institutional corset was not made for tackling a complex issue such as climate change or, more generally, the ecological emergencies we face:

- The corset's legal stays or bonings have been made during a time in which professional views on central banking had gone to neo-liberal extremes. Rather than striking a fine balance between central bank independence, democratic accountability, and the need to have arrangements for policy coordination between monetary and other (fiscal, quasi-fiscal, and structural) policies, the ECB statues are characterized by a radical emphasis on independence and inflation aversion. This hampers an integrated approach that takes into account the interdependencies between different public balance sheets, in particular those of national fiscal institutions, financial support facilities on the European level, and the EIB and other public banks (for an example for such an approach, see Murau 2020).
- The corset's ideological fabric is an expression of a mix of Northern European and neoliberal views toward central banking. In the ECB's case, the legitimate concern to attenuate the dangers of unlimited money has been used to foster a neglect of the fact that monetary policy has distributional and structural consequences that require a holistic approach to policy. Ironically, this is especially apparent from recent cases brought to the European Court of Justice. By naively scandalizing the fiscal impact of monetary policy actions, the German plaintiffs have unintentionally put a spotlight on a simple fact: that fighting inflation or deflation always and everywhere has distributional consequences and that these require democratic control over monetary policy, a thing the same plaintiffs abhor.
- The corset's objective lacing has been strapped too tight. By operationalizing price stability at a level below 2% (or, in the case of pre-accession countries, 1.5%

below less than 2%) and by not operationalizing the secondary goals mentioned in the Treaties, policymakers have chosen to excessively limit the ECB's operating range. The same holds true for governance arrangements or concepts such as market neutrality.

What can be done to tailor a new corset for the ECB? Most proposals on greening central banking take the existing corset for granted (see Table 1); others largely ignore it and hope for a change of the Treaties or a completely revamped set-up of the monetary union. In the first case, the resulting proposals are often rather timid and thus not adequate to the challenge of climate change. Alternatively, they accept to hand over control over a largely fiscal and structural area to nonelected officials. In the second case, projects might be bolder but would require a lengthy process of institutional change not consistent with the urgency of the problem. In particular, current governance arrangements in and around the ECB are insufficient to ensure the needed coordination. Moreover, the eurozone does not have established procedures and cultural practice of coordination. A strategy that wants to green the ECB needs to take these issues of the institutionalization of macro-financial policies, in particular their relationship to each other, into account.

Such a program confronts two main challenges. First, it is unclear whether a new institutionalization of monetary policy requires changes to EU Treaties, which are generally expected to be highly unlikely. Many observers therefore hope that greening the ECB more radically can be done within the boundaries of the current legal set-up, without touching the Treaties. Others feel it will be necessary to engage in a fundamental overhaul of the Union's monetary constitution. We will return to this problem in Sect. 4, by presenting a proposal that, in our view, stretches the limits of the legal foundations of the ECB, but does not violate them. We emphasize that our assessment is not based on a judicial but a common-sense economic reading of the Treaties, hoping to inspire legal scholars to join the debate.

Second, attempts to institutionalize a transformative ECB creates understandable fears to open Pandora's Box, in the sense of making the ECB a playing field for a diverse set of political interests or even a political football. Many observers, not only but particularly in Germany, believe that central banks should be exclusively about fighting inflation, and not be burdened with a transformative or developmental role. Both would not only require compromises with respect to price stability but also imply a loss of independence not consistent with macroeconomic stability. The kind of democratic embeddedness needed for engaging in an explicit support of a political program of structural, socio-ecological changes is not acceptable for these observers. Recent decades have made these views mainstream (see the latter part of the next section). Increasingly, however, the view that central banks should be exclusively about fighting inflation and should enjoy a rather extreme form of independence has been questioned. Some authors such as Epstein (2013) describe the recent departure from a more developmental, political central bank as the exception rather than the rule. What lessons does history offer on the consequences and nature of such forms of "transformative central banking"?

3 Context and Constant Struggles: Transformative Central Banking

Recent historical research invites us to think about the relationship between broader economic transformations and central bank practices. Central banks are described as subjects and objects of transformation. In our view, this research allows us to draw a number of conclusions, which can be sketched out as follows, and will be developed hereafter:

1. *Central banking has evolved in a sometimes steady, and other times turbulent, fashion, but its evolution has always reflected and shaped the larger transformations of the socioeconomic context.* Its objectives, operations, roles, and governance cannot be understood without reference to "domestic political economies" (Ugolini 2017) and the macro-regime or state systems these economies operate in (Klüh 2015). Due to this contextual nature, it is inadequate to think about central banks as organizations that just target inflation and ensure financial stability. It is also naïve to assume that formal mandates hamper central banks' ability to adopt to new circumstances (Posen 2010). Rather, shifts in the global policy agenda as well as in economic and political power balances of a currency area will change central banking practices and their legal foundations, though it is unclear which change will dominate the interplay between operational realities and the law.
2. *The double nature of central banks as organizations that form an integral part of the political and the financial system defines the way in which practices adopt to a changing context.* These roles are mediated through state money. Central banks use their status as state institutions to preserve their privileged position aloof from other financial institutions. At the same time, they need their status within the financial sector to defend against excessive political interference (Posen 1995). Presenting the evolution of central banks vis-à-vis other state actors obscures its evolution vis-à-vis finance, and vice versa. To understand central banking, it is necessary to overcome the usual state-market dichotomy, to conceive markets as entities that have to be organized socially and politically, and to understand the modern state as a reflection of market societies.[4]
3. *Describing central banks in a contextual manner should not disguise the constant struggles they face.* These struggles are expressions of their unique position. In contrast to positions held by researchers from "Modern Monetary Economics," they require a logical distinction between a monetary and a fiscal sphere of statehood. The fiscal sphere is characterized by democratic deliberation and a

[4]Readers interested in the methodological foundations of such a conception are referred to the analytical program of the so-called Économie des conventions (for an introduction, see Diaz-Bone 2015). Here, the social and political organization of markets is transformed through an ongoing dispute between plural orders for the common good or "conventions" (Boltanski and Thévenot 2018). At the center of the analytical interest are the statistical control techniques for the installation of markets, which are not understood here as neutral, but historically and politically controversial.

desire to keep track of the future obligations of the state. The monetary sphere is characterized by a mix between independence from and accountability to democratic deliberation. It reflects the need to moderate a system in which the state's ability to create legal tender is technically and necessarily boundless. While state money emerges as a consequence of the sameness of fiat currency and public debt, its workings require a distinction between the two.

4. *When democratic modes of governance dominate and public accountability can be assumed, different degrees of central bank independence are consistent with stable economic development.* The constitutive role of central banks meant that they assumed the task of having to supply a set of public goods (requiring democratic control) and a fictitious commodity (requiring a certain independence from democratic control). The mix of public goods changed over time but may best be described as "supporting economic development" including lowering the interest rates on loans, universalizing legal tender, and smoothening the economic cycle. On top, central banks had to safeguard the premise that the use of a state-based and uniform credit money fulfills a core function in capitalist development, enabling and entering the accumulation process.

We go over to flesh out the reasoning behind such an account in highlighting some historical constants and contexts.

Economists' views on the evolution of central banks have long been dominated by Goodhart's account of their emergence, which focuses on the central bank as part of the financial system and banking community (Goodhart 1985).[5] Goodhart's starting point is the growing academic trend to question the rationale for central banks that started in the 1970s. This trend builds upon earlier research on "free banking," both from the nineteenth century and the 1930s (Smith and Yeager 1990). Goodhart intends to show that there is a "natural" historical tendency toward a central institution. By legitimizing a departure from a free market solution, he constitutes a private solution as the reference case. Central banks emerge from their role as guarantor of stability in an otherwise unstable, bank-dominated financial system. Even after their full-fledged institutionalization, they are not seen as public or state institutions per se, but as noncompetitive, nonprofit-maximizing entities. The fact that these entities have been established by state legislation is a consequence of the difficulties that come up in the course of the transition from a member of the banking community to a primus inter pares and finally to the regulatory control center.

The latest empirical research on the history of central banks (see Battilossi et al. (2020), Chaps. 33–37) has recently called this narrative into question by showing the deeper involvement of public policies, political economies, and state-like actors in the monetary system. Ugolini (2020) denies the existence of an "evolution" altogether, emphasizing the diversity of institutional equilibria in different regions and during different times. There is neither a "survival of the fittest" nor a "one-size-fits

[5]We are mainly referring to the economics literature on central bank history, as we are not only interested in actual but also in.

all" institutional arrangement nor a "holy grail" (Needham 2020). When it comes to deconstructing the historical emergence of central banks, their role for banking (emphasized by Goodhart) is often dominated by their more general role as a public agent pursuing a variety of (often) explicit policy objectives. Bindseil (2019), for example, analyzes the constitutions of several European banks before 1800 which had not earned the batch of a central bank in the common reception yet. He shows that they fulfilled central banking functions even before the foundation of the Bank of England and the Swedish Riksbank which are usually referred to as the first central banks. What sticks out in their institutional experiences is that these banks had, what you today would call, a developmental mission. They were not merely a source of war finance or a lender of last resort, but a strategic element in the emergence of modern statehood. As a consequence, a diverse set of complex governance arrangements emerged, featuring representatives of the public sector, the trading sector and financiers.

Taken together, the two strands of economic research on central bank history leave us with a highly chimeric depiction of central banks as hybrids of finance and state, a depiction also backed by other accounts such as Paniagua (2021). They are state institutions mostly represented by financial sector representatives; they combine features of a company and a public administration, operate through concomitant participation in and regulation of markets, and are seen as representative of a real and a financial logic. They make profits, though they are nonprofit entities; they facilitate the impositions of markets and protect against such impositions; they protect both Main Street and Wall Street, though the first sees the latter as the main cause of the need for protection. How is it possible that such a conflicting and paradoxical entity enjoys such a broad reputation and credibility that makes it the source of much of the trust in capitalist modes of accumulation? More concretely, how can we explain society's trust in an institution that is part of two spheres that society often distrusts, the state and the financial system?

The analysis in Polanyi (1944) is a useful starting point to resolve that puzzle. Polanyi describes the emergence of market societies as a series of commodification processes for land, labor, and money. Central banks fortified this process from early on, but in the nineteenth century, the commodification of money suddenly changed its nature. Growing industrial production and infrastructural demands called for combining the credit function of money for the development of markets, with the logic of international trade and the use of metallic money. The drive toward realizing the commodity fiction then created the sometimes competing aims of developing a credit function to make money operable toward more uses while limiting it to make it operable along more geographies. The institutional experience of central banks in Europe, as also elaborated by Goodhart (1985), mirrors these conflicting lines: Territorialization often posed a challenge to the establishment of a central bank, as did conflicts over the question who should be able to draw on the credit function of the monetary system, and who shouldn't.

A Polanyian reading of central bank history indicates that the chimeric nature of central banking and its development over time is a reflection of its role in the double movement that characterizes the emergence of market societies (Savevska 2019).

Polanyi's account of monetary history is consistent with a view that describes central banks as "double agents" of the financial system and the public sector.[6] In modern societies that have largely completed the transformation from communities ("Gemeinschaft") to a functionally differentiated society ("Gesellschaft") (Dale 2008), this double agency is one between the economic and the political system. On the one hand, the central bank's legitimacy vis-à-vis society is founded on the protection of society against the impositions of the markets, in particular the financial markets.[7] On the other hand, the central bank also draws legitimacy from its role in protecting financial markets against a state that, from time to time, abuses its ability to issue currency or draw on the ability of banks to create credit.

Their dual protective function puts the central bank in a delicate position. In tranquil times, both the political and the financial sphere respect this position and do their best to support it, which is also times in which the central bank's power remains uncontested. Whenever (financial) markets gain a social role that exceeds the central bank's capacity to control them (a process often called financialization) or whenever the state develops authoritarian structures that exceed the central bank's capacity to defend against it, the delicate balance is destroyed. The central bank falls prey to one of its two symbionts. In Polanyian terms, the first process can be described as a dis-embedding of markets from society. The second one often constitutes the destructive variant of re-embedding, in which radical populist ideologies falsely promise to bring back sovereign control over markets. Paradoxically, the fear of such destructive dis-embedding often stands behind institutionalizations of central banking that favor financialization and, as a consequence, radicalization. With the aim to insulate central banks from authoritarian pressures, their function as protective shield is being ignored, also due to the fact that the interests supporting this role have been weakened through marketization. Constructive forms of re-embedding therefore increase democratic control over central banking, which is therefore not to be feared. In fact, democratic control is a precondition for allowing a certain amount of independence.

Up until the nineteenth century, central bank governance strongly reflects its dual nature, but it becomes more explicitly public over time. An important driver of this development is the fact that the universalization of money through the gold standard was state-led. Trying to acquire gold through trade during peace times and aiming for a boost in gold resources through war and colonization were a state task. At the same time, going to war meant that the credit function was regularly drawn upon, with respective effects in the case of losing the war or the dominion over colonies.

---

[6] In order to develop a theory of central banks as an adjunct but separate state institution, a politico-economic account is boiled down to an analytical distinction between "the financial sector" and "the state," the latter understood as being obliged to grant certain social and participatory rights.

[7] In financialized economic systems (those in which the logic and culture of the financial system start to dominate other economic logics, see Mader et al. 2020), this simple distinction becomes more complicated. The term "society" might then enclose segments of the economy that are positively connoted in society, such as the "Realwirtschaft" in Germany or "Main Street" in the USA.

Finally, the gold standard required close international cooperation of a kind that only nation-states could accomplish at the time. In parallel and looking more closely at the relationship between public and private influences through ownership and governance structures, the developments described by Goodhart (1985) in fact did play an important role in shaping governance: To ensure the containment of banking risks and the efficient management of informational problems within the financial sector, the Bank of England was developed as a noncompetitive, nonprofit-maximizing entity. Other countries then copied this arrangement and realized it much more smoothly by governmental legislation (Goodhart 1985, p. 104).

The twentieth century then triggered a series of events which finally institutionalized central banks' position as mediator between the financial markets and the state. On the one hand, the commodification process of labor created the need and the conditions for a strong political and economic representation of workers, resulting in a broadening of the labor movement. This triggered an institutionalization of new kinds of power relations in Europe: Liberal democracies, where they could be established, included social democratic parties in the parliament and labor unions, and their constitutions lent themselves not only to private sector freedoms but also to economic equality interests of these new social classes (Neumann 1942 [2018]). On the other hand, the commodification of money reached a new peak, and waves of financialization and de-financialization swept over economies. The two waves of globalization that accompanied financialization favored state and private actor strategies which served an external money function and not primarily an internal one (Pettifor 2019).

The Great Depression is the first watershed of this development. The period leading to the Great Depression can be described as a first wave of financialized disembedding of markets. A dominant feature of this wave is the way in which the gold standard and thus the external money function developed into a highly powerful and highly destructive force. Polanyi (1944 [2001]) describes in detail how central banks were becoming more and more desperate in their attempts to preserve the gold standard and serve as a cushion against its destructiveness (Clar 2019). The inability to combine these two roles finally played a crucial role in causing the bouts of hyperinflation in the beginning and the Great Depression toward the end of the 1920s. Interestingly and especially in the German context, these experiences are often seen as evidence for the dangers of firmly integrating monetary policy with the institutions of democratic decision-making. This view, however, does not only ignore the peculiar circumstances after the First World War, which would have brought every central bank however independent to the brink of disaster. It also pays inadequate attention to the actual institutionalization of monetary policy, in particular in Germany (Marsh 1992). And most importantly, it neglects the fact that the hyperinflations of the 1920s were not so much expressions of democracy but of desperate attempts to fulfill the Polanyian double role in the context of a Peace Treaty that made these impossible.

In reaction to the Great Depression, two forms of re-embedding were set into motion, a destructive and a constructive one. On the one hand, fascist regimes emerged, which abused the craving of parts of the population for protection from the global markets to put in place aggressive forms of nationalism. On the other hand, the New Deal policies of the Roosevelt administration attempted a democratic re-embedding of markets. As the first variant soon revealed its destructiveness (finally leading to the Second World War, the Holocaust, and a complete shattering of the world economic system), the second variant finally prevailed.

In its destructive variant, re-embedding led the central bank into the hands of autocratic regimes. Ironically, the fear of democratic control over central banks is often rooted in the experiences with such destructive re-embedding. One reason why the debate on "more influence of the state in central banking" often leads to a comparison with fascism in the German context is that National Socialism is understood as state command over the economy. This interpretation, though, is still contested. Scholars have argued that, for the most time, the Nazis left the private sector with a substantial degree of autonomy, and economic expansion went hand in hand with slashing labor rights. Neumann (1942 [2018]) shows that the initiative of the NSDAP to assume more control over the corporate sector was quickly put aside in favor of maintaining free enterprise in principle while introducing hierarchical elements to facilitate coordinated action. Similarly, the relationship between the emergence (see in particular Clar, 2019) and development (as described, for example, in Marsh 1992) of the Nazi regime and the institutions of German central banking proves to be much more complicated than often portrayed. By no means, they can serve as an indication that the danger of autocracy always and everywhere implies a need for maximum central bank independence.

In its constructive variant, re-embedding implied a partial but substantial democratization of central banks. In this respect, the US experience of the 1930s is exemplary. The New Deal did not only develop a focus on strengthening the organization of labor, while the corporate sector was put under control through general law, including the well-known regulations on banking. It also led to a radical departure from established views on macroeconomic policies. In particular in terms of monetary policy, Roosevelt and his team developed a rather radical view on the needed changes (Pettifor 2019), finally leading to the Gold Reserve Act of 1934.[8] Against the backdrop of the dismal performance of central banks in preventing the Great Depression, they were put in the "back seat" of policymaking.

Ultimately, the constructive variant of re-embedding prevailed in the form of the postwar consensus and the Bretton-Woods regime. This consensus, with all its problems in terms of its extractive nature and treatment of the Global South (Burawoy 2012), holds some important lessons for the institutionalization of the financial sector in general and central banking in particular. Most importantly, the developments from the Second World War to the 1970s show that limited central bank independence and strong restrictions on finance do not necessarily lead to either an abandonment of democracy or hyperinflation. Financial markets and organizations were mostly instituted as mere infrastructures for more important economic players, namely, real sector enterprises, unions, and finance ministries

[8] On public spending, Roosevelt uphold a number of quite orthodox views, which according to some limited the New Deal in its effectiveness (Lehndorff 2020).

(Hütten and Klüh 2017). The internal functions of money dominated, reflecting rather strong limits to international capital mobility. Central banks were given a limited degree of autonomy, with substantial differences among the respective economic systems. Coordination between different macroeconomic policies was seen as key, to be able to deliver on a multiplicity of economic policy goals, very much in contrast to the focus on inflation and growth that has dominated recent decades. But none of these developments did lead to autocracy or a complete loss of monetary stability.

With the abandonment of the Bretton Woods system, a new wave of financialization was set into motion, accompanied by a new and radicalized version of central bank independence. Parallel to a reincarnation of ideas such as "free banking," the political codetermination of monetary and fiscal policies was replaced by a system in which an independent central bank would form the center of gravity of macroeconomic policy. Western states settled on a monetary order with flexible exchange rates and high capital mobility, the logic which in some ways resembles that of the gold standard. As a key element, the concept of inflation targeting took center stage. While the move toward a new paradigm of monetary control first proceeded slowly, it gained surprising strength in the 1990s. For example, in 1988, a proponent of central bank independence such as Alberto Alesina would carefully frame:

> This paper argues tentatively that independent Central Banks have been associated with a lower average inflation rate and may have been responsible for reducing politically induced volatility of monetary policy and inflation. (Alesina 1988, 845)

In the middle of the 1990s, this carefulness would have been replaced by much stronger statements, such as:

> Particularly the independence of the central bank—which had not been a major topic of academic discussion for a long time either—has since become the nucleus of a positive and normative theory of inflation. The fact that there is a close connection between the independence of the central bank and success in the field of combating inflation can be justified convincingly not only in theory. Empirical evidence is conclusive, too: . . . At the same time, the fact that high and volatile inflation rates are associated with high costs for the overall economy and that stable prices are conducive to the long-term growth process are, in my opinion, two of the established findings of our discipline. (Issing 2019, 289)

And toward the end of the 1990s, even more progressive observers such as Dornbusch would boldly subscribe to the view that:

> The idea of a political body that interacts with the ECB is shocking: Europe and the world have moved a healthy distance from short-term political control of monetary policy. (Dornbusch et al. 1998, 28)

The ECB is by far the most radical expression of the views on independence that developed since the 1980s. Three factors came together to boost the general trend toward independence in the case of the ECB. First, German resistance to a monetary union could only be overcome by agreeing to a set of institutions that cemented the orthodox views of the Bundesbank and the German economic orthodoxy (Needham 2020). Second, the lack of a framework for European fiscal policy created a vacuum of control that could not be filled otherwise, at least not in a democratic fashion. Third, European societies embarked on a trend that was later coined "financialization." This trend, which is described in detail in Mader et al. (2020), embodies a view of central banking very strongly centered on their role for financial markets, their technocratic competency, and their detachment from government.

The financial crisis of 2008 highlighted the fragility of a financialized economy and has set into motion modern versions of the two variants of re-embedding described above. On the one hand, developments such as Brexit, the Trump presidency, and the rise of autocratic regimes demonstrate the continuous importance of the false association between a protection from the hardships of global markets and finance and nationalistic tendencies. On the other hand, the idea of a socio-ecological transformation that combines the need for a more sustainable economy with the call for a more inclusive economy has gained in importance. The current debates on the future of central bank independence reflect these developments. On the one hand, autocratic regimes threaten their central banks with interference if they do not support their policy agenda. On the other hand, proponents of Green Deals and Green New Deals see monetary policy as a way to speed up the transition to a more sustainable society.

Against this backdrop, it is likely that the institutionalization of central banking will change in the years to come, hopefully in favor of a policy agenda determined by democratic politics. More concretely, both forms of re-embedding would reduce the scope of central bank independence vis-à-vis governments. At the same time, central banks are likely to remain entities that stand between the world of finance and the world of the political and defend their partial independence against both worlds. Their exact fate, however, will strongly depend on which of the two forms of re-embedding will prevail. They will either be democratized or instrumentalized, and much should be done to redress the balance in the direction of the former. In contrast, radical views of a complete abolishment of the distinction between a fiscal and a monetary sphere, often voiced under the heading of "Modern Monetary Economics," are unlikely to prevail. They are legitimate expressions of a discomfort with financialization, extreme central bank independence, and unnecessary limits to collective action, but they underestimate the need for complex institutional arrangements that position central banks in between the financial and the political sphere while ensuring democratic governance. Even doubtful observers such as Pixley (2018) maintain a hope for democratic central banking, though they are skeptical about the continuous influence of financial actors and the agenda of elected policymakers. With this in mind, she rightly points out that institutional arrangements for central banks are important but that the decisive question is about the degree of democratic governance of the overall political system and the control of vested interests. In the current situation, this means reflecting about the relationship between capitalism and democracy (Sturn et al. 2019). The financial sector, with its continuously strong presence of public entities, would be a natural starting point for a renewed democratization of the economy (Klüh 2021) and the central bank a natural starting point to initiate this process.

Re-democratized central banks with partial independence can play a very useful role in the transition to a sustainable economy. Financial markets and institutions play a key role in most political strategies to achieve an ecological transformation (Land 2019a). The future development of sustainable finance and its potential to contribute to the success of national, European, and global climate policies, however, depends on the interplay between distinct spheres: the private financial sector; the public financial sector including developmental, promotional, and public banks, the so-called real economy; and the noneconomic, mainly political, sphere. As public entities that partly share the institutional logic of the financial sector more broadly, central banks will be a key player in orchestrating these spheres.

The historical accounts show that central banks are best conceived as public entities with mandates that are consistent with society's developmental agenda. This becomes apparent from the experience with early and later central banks. A single focus on inflation and extreme degrees of independence, however, is neither necessary nor sufficient conditions for functional monetary and financial system. In particular at the ECB, there is enough scope to reintegrate central banks into the democratic realm without giving up central bank independence altogether. The extreme versions of independence that emerged since the 1970s are neither consistent with the historical accounts on central bank performance, nor with democratic principles, nor with a healthy and sustainable level of independence in the long run. Stiglitz (2001), in his foreword for the 2001 edition of Polanyi's *The Great Transformation*, highlights this view in the following quote:

> The disjunction between these more basic values [those highlighted by Polanyi] and the ideology of the self-regulated market is as clear today as it was at the time he wrote. We tell developing countries about the importance of democracy, but then, when it comes to the issues they are most concerned with, those that affect their livelihoods, the economy, they are told: the iron laws of economics give you little or no choice; and since you (through your democratic political process) are likely to mess things up, you must cede key economic decisions, say concerning macroeconomic policy, to an independent central bank, almost always dominated by representatives of the financial community; and to ensure that you act in the interest of the financial community, you are told to exclusively focus on inflation...

Today, the focus of the debate on central bank governance is shifting, from inflation targeting and increased independence to multiple goals and democratic governance. The preceding analysis shows that the democratic backing of central banks is highly contextual. Since the 1970s, the context has been one of neoliberal reform and financialization, two interdependent processes of social change. As a consequence, and in line with ideals of technocratic governance, central banks were distanced from the rest of government. Moreover, their responsibilities, agendas and processes have been aligned with the needs of the financial sector, sometimes in a responsible way, often excessively. In some cases, central banks have become market-makers of last resort, a legitimate role if the premises of financialization are accepted. In others, they themselves have illegitimately pursued an agenda of radical financialization of society. In this case, central banks have not only been delegitimized but openly financialized. To adhere rigidly to concepts such as "market neutrality" is an expression of such financialization. Independent from the exact nature of their financialization and in parallel to it, central banks have been successively distanced from the rest of the public sector and re-focused on fighting inflation.

Large-scale socioeconomic transformations have been episodes in which the institutionalization and organization of central banking change, too. Periods of a dis-embedding of markets are usually associated with a more autonomous monetary and financial sphere, periods of re-embedding with a realignment with the general political sphere. Whether such re-alignment proved to be socially beneficial or not has been largely a function of the nature of the underlying transformation. In antidemocratic transformations such as the one experienced in Europe during the 1930s, making the central bank an object of the government can have disastrous consequences. In transformations that aim at strengthening democratic politics, including through keeping market outcomes in check and adjusting them in line with the majority's views, outcomes have been mixed but generally in line with intentions. More concretely, there have been negative side effects such as higher inflation, but the more important goals have been reached, such as financing the war effort against Nazi Germany in the context of the USA and its allies, re-building economies after World War II, or stabilizing unstable economies at high employment levels in the years between the 1940s and the 1970s.

In a nutshell, the historical experience seems to indicate that we do need to fear the coexistence of autocracy and central bank dependence, not democratic control over central banks. At the same time, the coexistence between a formal democracy and an excessive monetary independence can also be hazardous, as it might lead to the kind of socioeconomic instability experienced during the Great Depression of the 1920s and the Great Recession of the early twenty-first century. In contrast, there are few examples of bad policy outcomes when limits to central bank independence are set in an environment of democratization and stable institutions. Importantly, this statement presumes a serene attitude toward a certain level of inflation. We believe that such an attitude is backed by the literature, which generally shows that inflation in the single digits is usually consistent with growth and development, in particular when combined with measures to protect vulnerable groups from its consequences, through direct and indirect indexation of transfer incomes as well as strong unions to protect real wages.

It is worth highlighting that our reading of history seems to contradict four other influential views on the relation between the central bank and the rest of the public sector:

- Some proponents of Modern Monetary Theory deny that differentiating between the monetary sphere and the rest of government is warranted at all. They argue that the only relevant distinction is the difference between responsible and irresponsible macro-financial policies.
- Proponents of radical forms of central bank independence simply deny the existence of periods in which society has benefitted from a closer alignment between the central bank and the rest of government. Usually, such views come

with a strong aversion against inflation and/or fears that compromising central bank independence is a route to an excessively powerful state.

- Others regard limited independence combined with democracy as being a recipe for problems, too, independent of the political context. These views are largely based on theoretical arguments of time-inconsistent policies and a general distrust toward political interference with the macroeconomy.
- Still others agree that democratic control over central banking might be beneficial but should be avoided to guard against a change in government. If the power to create money changes hands from a democratic to an autocratic regime, one would have wished to have a little less democratic control over money at the outset, the argument goes.

We would argue that the first two arguments are not backed by historical experience: Especially the decades after the Great Depression have shown that government control over money and macroeconomic stability can go hand in hand. At the same time, numerous examples illustrate the fragility of fiat money systems to capture, both from financial and from political personnel (Pixley 2018). After all and on top of the Polanyian argument presented above, capitalism has to live with a fundamental monetary paradox: It only works when money is scarce and abundant at the same time. Money has to be scarce to reproduce capitalisms' behavioral and informational foundations. Money has to be abundant to enable its defining Schumpeterian core, the dynamism with which resources can be divested and invested. In this situation, pressures to ease the consequences of scarce money will naturally make use of its endless availability. The distinction between the monetary and the fiscal sphere is key to moderate these pressures.

It is for these reasons that the third and the fourth arguments have to be taken seriously. While much of the third argument is made on theoretical grounds, it is at least partly based on the experiences of the 1970s. However, it seems that a short-lived bout of inflation during that time has excessively influenced our views on the matter. It is understandable that researchers in the 1980s have focused on the dangers of inflationary policies in democratic societies, but in the grand theme of things, these dangers seem to have been overrated. While it is indeed true that democratic pressures to use monetary policy to solve distributional problems can become overwhelming, social mobilization will also produce counter-pressures as soon as inflation becomes a real problem. In the short term, to cite Issing, inflation might indeed share some characteristics of toothpaste, as it is difficult to get it back into the tube. Over longer terms, however, the cost of keeping too much toothpaste in the tube might well be higher than wasting some of it for the benefit of your teeth.

3.1 Steps Toward a Sustainable and Transformative ECB

The aim of this section is to provide the sketch of a "strategy" to make the ECB a transformative agent with a serious ambition toward sustainability and greening the economy while trying to avoid the pitfalls of existing proposals: First, instead of looking at all functions of the ECB, from banking supervision to macro-financial stability all the way up to monetary policy, we restrict ourselves to the latter. Even though we recognize the need to follow a more holistic and integrated approach in the end, we believe that such a narrow focus is warranted. By zooming in on monetary policy including its operational dimension, one can demonstrate that a consistent approach will require an integration of new goals, new instruments, and new governance arrangements and thus a complete overhaul of eurozone arrangements.

Second, rather than accepting or ignoring the fact that the ECB's current legal, ideational, and operational corset is too tight for the purpose on hand, we intend to widen it. To do so, we stretch the corset to the extent that we believe is possible under the Treaties. As we do not belong to the legal profession, we sometimes advance rather radical, political interpretations of the Treaty language. We thus follow a strongly constructionist approach: Rather than (legal) originalism, we favor textualism or, better, contextualism, in the sense of allowing principles to vary with the historical context. We believe that this is not only warranted but necessary, as current views on the ECB's mandate and governance have been evolved path-dependently from the very radical views on central bank independence and inflation prevailing in the 1990s.

Third, we take into account, as far as this is possible in a highly uncertain environment, the current macroeconomic and political challenges resulting from the aftermath of the pandemic, the current war in Ukraine, and the fact that planetary boundaries and the finiteness of natural and atmospheric resources are increasingly priced, with ensuing consequences for inflation dynamics. In particular, we recognize the need for the ECB to react flexibly in a very volatile environment while consistently and constantly fighting climate change. This has several consequences. First, and foremost, it requires giving the ECB sufficient policy space and discretion to follow up on secondary policy goals: The ECB's engagement in climate policy cannot pause just because inflation runs at 2.5%, 4%, or 6%, a development that is clearly possible, given the size of shocks we are observing. This, in our view, implies moving to an inflation target range, a range that has to be reached over the medium term.

Second, the shocks we have been seeing recently are part of a larger story, in which the finiteness of the planet becomes a stronger factor in political and macroeconomic developments. Partly as a consequence of policies aiming at internalizing environmental costs, partly in anticipation of future scarcity, markets are increasingly pricing in this finiteness. This might lead to a period of, on average, higher inflation. It might also likely lead to more inflation variability. Against this backdrop, monetary policy does not only need additional discretionary elements but sufficient policy independence. The time in which one inflation rate could be considered more or less right for extended periods might be over.

Third, financing public and private investments for a greening of the economy might face stronger headwinds when long-term interest rates adjust to the new environment. New expenditures abound, for example, as a consequence of geopolitical developments. Strong sovereigns like Germany have missed out on the opportunity to issue more debt at negative interest rates. They now might be confronted with new financing conditions that are less supportive for debt-financed large public investment in sustainable infrastructures. Sovereigns like Italy might face renewed fiscal pressures exactly when large investments are needed. Central banks will need to take this into account when setting rates and choosing other measures, as the dynamics of climate change do not allow a prolonged period of consolidation to precede the massive public investments needed.

In short, European climate and environmental policy only has a small window of opportunity to take action that is radical enough to decarbonize and green the European economy. On top, the political and economic context presents unexpected challenges. These challenges require both a highly functional central bank that enjoys sufficient policy and operational independence and a bold move toward "democratically embedded central banking" (Dezernat Zukunft 2020). We recognize the need for some form of policy, operational and financial independence, but propose to provide the ECB with clearer guidelines as well as governance and coordination arrangements with respect to its role in the socio-ecological transformation. To square this circle and allow the ECB to contribute to climate policy in such an environment, we propose a three-pronged strategy. Each prong is related to one of the ECB's roles in economic policymaking:

- The first prong views the ECB as an entity enjoying a certain degree of necessary and justified policy independence. To be able to use its broad set of instruments freely while contributing to the greening of the European economy, however, goal independence has to give way. More concretely, we believe that both the specification of price stability and the prioritization and operationalization of secondary goals should be a responsibility of lawmakers. Moreover, the degree to which primary and secondary objectives have been reached should be regularly monitored by lawmakers. This requires, in our view, an overhaul of accountability arrangements.
- The second prong considers the ECB as an entity whose actions and instruments need to be consequentially aligned with the Green Deal and the EU taxonomy while leaving enough room for operational independence. The ECB has to decide on the details of greening its operations, from the rules on collateral to the nature of its asset purchases. But it also needs clear guidelines as to how consequentially and how quickly this should take place and how these changes are to be coordinated with other agents of the transformation. Moreover, while changes to collateral rules and asset purchases appear to be rather technical, they have sizeable quasi-fiscal and structural consequences for which the ECB lacks legitimacy. While some of these consequences can be monitored within the realm of standard but overhauled accountability arrangements, others require more extensive coordination with other bodies of the executive or the public financial sector. In the latter cases, this coordination would require setting up (democratically controlled) coordinating bodies, in which strategies, tactics, and operations of the

financial dimension of the European Green Deal are discussed, decided, and monitored.

- The third prong considers the ECB as an entity that has the ability to carry out fiscal policies per pro of the sovereigns in the monetary union as well as the European Union. To make sure that the risks of such actions do not impair financial independence, clear rules and arrangements are necessary. As a fiscal agent, the ECB needs to be even more closely aligned with the policies agreed upon in a coordinated fashion. Consequently, they would be part of the elaborations in new coordinating bodies and monitored accordingly.

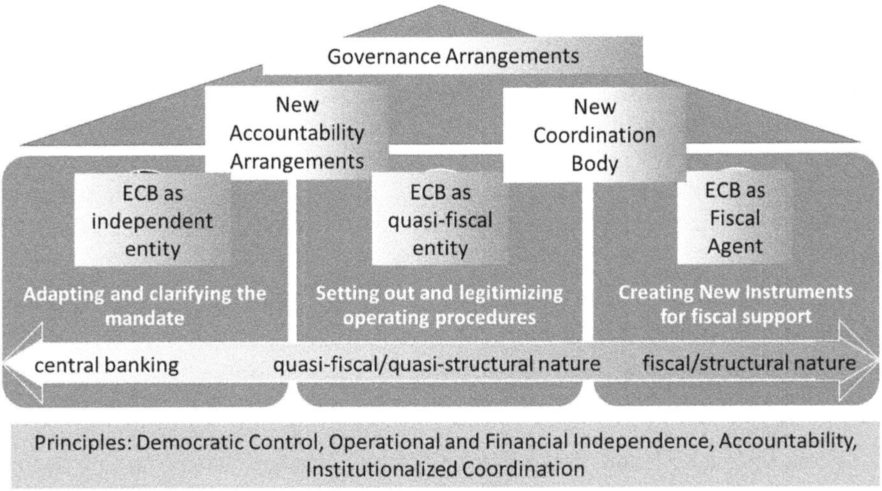

Prong I: Adapting and Clarifying the Mandate

For the ECB as an entity enjoying policy independence (which largely focuses on what the literature calls central banking, i.e., steering liquidity and financial conditions so that certain macroeconomic objectives are reached), we propose an adaptation and clarification of the mandate. More concretely, we suggest three institutional innovations, all at the initiative and under the auspices of the European legislative. The latter would:

1. Clarify the primary mandate by defining and regularly re-defining the range for price stability, in consultation with an expert council consisting of representatives of the ECB, academia, and civil society. As a basis for the discussion, we suggest to define price stability as "an increase in consumer prices of not less than 1.5 and not more than 3.5 percent over the medium term, taking into account the inflationary consequences of the socio-ecological transformation resulting from climate change, decarbonization and a broader greening of the economy."

2. Clarify, along the lines of the Green Deal, the secondary mandate by prioritizing and operationalizing those objectives and take into account whenever the primary objective is met.
3. Increase the grip of accountability arrangements, by, at a minimum, implementing the proposals laid down in Claeys and Domínguez-Jiménez (2020, p. 1), including "procedural changes to the Monetary Dialogue to increase its effectiveness" and "the release of detailed minutes and votes from ECB governing council meetings."

The three measures would constitute a bold and straightforward way to reinstate the primacy of democratic politics over central banking and accommodate the shift in the macro-regime. Moreover, they would be a very strong signal of the new priorities of the envisioned macro-regime, avoiding the current logic in which price stability can never be seen as fulfilled. Also, they are in line with earlier proposals to increase the effectiveness of monetary policy against the backdrop of the zero lower bound (Blanchard et al. 2010). Finally and surely to the surprise of many, we believe that the required changes might even be possible without a change in the Treaties. The second and third element of our proposal has already been advanced to the European Parliament, in a study requested by the ECON committee (Kern and Lastra 2020).

Implementing the first element, which is the most controversial one, will be a difficult political and technical challenge. Organizing a due process that combines political with scientific expertise is thus of the essence. For example, it will be necessary to disentangle the effects of desirable increases in prices of carbon-intensive and environmentally destructive economic activities from other inflationary developments. Closely related, distributional issues will need to be taken into account. At the same time, a constant discussion about the right inflation rate or range should be avoided. Against this backdrop, it might be sensible to work with a sunset clause, as suggested by Dezernat Zukunft (2020). The ECB would be given a clear operationalization of its primary mandate for a certain number of years, an operationalization that would then be subject to regular democratic elaboration.

It is also worth noting that a democratized operationalization of price stability would almost certainly face legal challenges, as the goal independence of ECB has been a holy grail of the European Monetary Union. Our (political) reading of the respective (legal) literature is that the ECB's right to define price stability itself stems from an assumption: That the fact that price stability is not defined in the Treaties implies that the ECB has the privilege of doing so. While this has certainly been the view and expectation during the signing of the Treaties, it remains an interpretation. In our view, the right of a subordinated entity such as the ECB to interpret a vague legal concept such as price stability only holds as long as the legislative chooses to leave it in a vague form. Should the EP and the Council decide to clarify the legal concept (e.g., because it is realized that the goal independence of the ECB is a rather unusual and radical construct from the heydays of neoliberalism or because there are urgent political reasons to constrict it), they can try doing so and still leave a final decision to the European Court of Justice. We even believe that our view that defining price stability is a responsibility of lawmakers and that 3.5% is a defendable level is indirectly backed by the Treaties. Particularly, it is in line with the convergence criteria specified in the Treaties by member countries and not the ECB. These define price stability as "a price performance that is sustainable and average inflation not more than 1.5 percentage points above the rate of the three best performing Member States." Taking the ECB's current definition of 2% seriously, this would imply price stability in a range up to 3.5%.[9] If the range we propose is deemed to be too conservative (many studies do not find any sizeable negative welfare effects of inflation below 5%), a reasonable alternative would be to choose 3.5% as the center of the range and 2 and 5% as its lower and upper limits.

With regard to the ECB's secondary objective, the European legislative needs to establish a process by which it operationalizes its political agenda insofar as it has implications for monetary policy. Despite the fact that it is the national governments' responsibility to spell out their economic policies properly, the established practice of coordinating and deciding on common EU policies and the current impetus to provide a political frame, such as the Green Deal and the sustainable finance agenda, already go in a similar direction. Claeys and Domínguez-Jiménez suggest that "[t]he European Parliament as representative of European citizens and the Council of the EU as representative of EU Member States should take the primary roles in determining the ranking of secondary objectives. As far as the EP is concerned, its resolution on the ECB's annual report would be a clear medium for the Parliament to make this ranking" (p. 23). Blot et al. (2021) and Reichlin et al. (2021) argue that the relationship between inflation and other objectives of economic policy should be regularly reviewed and enter the policy perspective, as many well-established relations have dissolved at the zero lower bound.

The clarification of the secondary mandate and its relevance for the ECB go hand in hand with tightening the cooperation between the central bank staff and legislative bodies. The legislative would increase its governance efforts by implementing proposals as laid down in Claeys and Domínguez-Jiménez (2020) or similar proposals. For example, it might be sensible to create a body from the parliament which is especially occupied with central banking issues. Chang and Hodson (2019) call for both the Monetary and Economic Dialogues to be delegated to a new ECON Euro Area Oversight Subcommittee (EAOS).

Prong II: Setting Out and Legitimizing Operating Procedures

The discussion on sustainable operating procedures and on the appropriate way of greening ECB instruments has been at the core of the debate on a more transformative ECB (see below, as well as Table 1 in the appendix). It has also been a rather technical discourse. On one side, there are good reasons to acknowledge the complex nature of the subject matter. Determining how a specific instrument or procedure should be adjusted to best support the objective of a more sustainable economy

[9] Currently, the ECB defines what "best performing" means and takes the three lowest inflation rates within the Eurozone. It then adds 1.5%. During the period of lowflation in recent years, this has led to an absurdly low convergence criterion.

requires taking into account a large number of potential mechanisms and unintended consequences, for example, on financial stability, and require a detailed examination of difficult questions:

- How strongly would market participants react to the different measures, also when considering the likely interaction effects between different policies? The answer to this question is much less clear than many expect. For example, an apparently strong measure such as additional haircuts for brown assets might have much less of an effect than expected, because these haircuts are intended to help manage short-term liquidity risks, not the type of medium to long-term risks associated with planetary boundaries.
- How does the effect of a certain measure depend on the action of other players? For example, using eligibility requirements might have a relatively strong effect, as the markets might interpret ECB rules as indicative for the future development of industry standards. However, this would require coordinating the actions of the ECB with those of the commission, other regulatory bodies, and standard setters, a coordination that might be complicated.
- Could a consequential application of sustainability rules have the effect that those companies are cut off the market that need green finance most desperately, because they belong to the so-called "brown" industries? Finding measures that do not only benefit the "best in class" but also those that need to adjust most is particularly tricky, as similar experiences in the area of sustainable finance suggest.

Answering these questions is of the essence but highly challenging. Quantification of effects and side effects is severely complicated by a lack of data, which might require an extended period of phasing in, data collection, and learning. This might also be necessary for reasons of financial stability. Getting the answers wrong might not only render the greening exercise ineffective but also cause abrupt market movements that endanger financial stability.

The mentioned complexities suggest leaving the decision of when and how to green what instrument to the experts within the ECB. However, letting the ECB do the job alone is not possible, for three reasons. Most importantly, the technical nature of the instruments should not conceal the fact that their application has substantial distributional and structural effects. These, in turn, require a political backing. The latter is also required because the effectiveness of a certain change will strongly depend on the actions of actors outside the ECB. For example, and as mentioned above, using new eligibility requirements works through helping an emerging standard of sustainability accounting and measurement to gain ground. The idea is to let ECB procedures be the stick and carrot that leads market participants to adopt the standard. The standard itself, however, would not be set by the ECB, but by different bodies, in particular the commission.

Greening instruments and procedures is thus a highly technical and a highly political issue. To deal with this tension, we propose to clearly delineate the responsibilities of the ECB and its counterparts whenever possible but create coordination arrangements in others: EU lawmakers would advise the ECB to consequentially adopt all its instruments to the exigencies of the Green Deal, with the final aim of making the ECB fully conformant with the EU Taxonomy and other rules. The exact nature and timing of operational changes would be determined by ECB staff and reported regularly to EPs. At the same time, an independent expert group would prepare regular reports on the ecological, structural, social, and fiscal impact of ECB operations.[10]

Put differently, we suggest that the ECB as a quasi-fiscal entity would spell out itself and, with a large degree of operational independence, the way in which it intends to support secondary objectives. In particular, it would develop taxonomy-based rules for greening the collateral pool and asset purchases as well as reforming eligibility requirements. However, it would take these decisions based on clear guidelines on what to achieve by when, and it would be monitored accordingly. Such monitoring would also involve public deliberations of situations in which a deviation from the ECB's plan of phasing in sustainable collateral and investment rules would be necessary, should the primary mandate require such deviation.

We believe that the EU's sustainable finance taxonomy is the right basis and vanishing point for such phasing in. One of the major mechanisms through which the ECB can support the socio-ecological transformation is by supporting the mainstreaming of general rules for what an economic entity should do and is allowed to do. Applying the taxonomy re-politicizes monetary policy decisions to a certain extent, as decisions on what counts as green are made in a political process rather than an ex-post tilting of the central bank. Taking such a reversed order in monetary policies seriously—which means to acknowledge the fiscal element in it—also has further implications: Steering economic activity according to the taxonomy transgresses a policy regime which is only centered on inflation targeting to one in which environmental factors actually count. Rather than judging this development as problematic, we see it fitting in the transformation of capitalism which is currently taking place.

Using the common rules is therefore necessary, even though they still have major caveats: To start with, many observers find it misleading that many carbon-intensive sectors are included, apparently motivated by the fact that reductions are expected in these areas. Moreover, there is no negative or blacklist for economic activities which could also inform central banking policies. As an alternative, Dafermos et al. (2020) use the Climate Policy Relevant Sectors (CPRS) classification. Along these lines, we suggest to apply an extended version of the taxonomy to the collateral pool and QE operations, as this establishes a clear hierarchy within the ECB's secondary mandate and leaves the ECB room to provide a proper implementation strategy. Since unconventional monetary policies have become the rule rather than the exception, the ECB needs to have a well-defined set of tools from which to choose from and which are in support of the general economic policies of the EU, including the Green

[10]To ensure a continued financial independence of the ECB, arrangements to deal with the potential losses related to concentrated investments in certain sectors might be necessary. One possibility would be to set up a fund that pockets parts of the profits from monetary operations and compensates the ECB in case of major market disturbances.

Deal and the goals of the Paris Agreement. That such a well-defined, but contingent plan, is necessary is underlined by a recent study published by the European Parliament: the authors suggest that a "new normal" has been prevalent before the outbreak of the COVID-19 pandemic already and that implications for monetary and fiscal policies are yet too little recognized (Demertzis and Domínguez-Jiménez 2020).

Apart from that, our proposal is very much in line with the two scenarios developed by Dafermos et al. (2020, 2021). They apply the taxonomy to the collateral pool and allow the central bank to provide lending in line with the climate impact relative to value added, and then increasingly purchase collateral from green and non-carbon-intensive investments. In their more ambitious version, they extend eligibility to green projects not covered by the current collateral pool yet. An alternative policy is developed by Oustry et al. 2020 who suggest a tilting—or alignment—approach including a climate-hedging portfolio approach. Here, the central bank aims to adapt its collateral policies toward the overall emission path of the economy rather than applying a one-by-one classification of assets (see also Schoenmaker (2021) and Hauser (2021)). Schnabel (2021) expresses sympathy for the latter strategy, as the former would lack an incentive structure for the higher polluting sectors. We would expect that a well-communicated phasing in of purchases from the taxonomy-conform collateral pool by the central bank does provide a sufficient incentive structure: Firms will know when their financing condition will tighten up but will have time to implement reduction strategies. At the same time, the central bank will be able to show how it balances financial market stability with risks stemming from the environmental crisis. A similar combination of phasing in and monitoring was outlined in a recent discussion paper by the Bank of England (Hauser 2021).

In a similar vein, the taxonomy should be applied to and used within the asset purchase programs, which—due to their carbon-bias and secondary effects on price developments—have already been discussed quite extensively. These discussions can serve as starting points for the deliberations within the ECB. For example, Ferrari and Landi (2020) suggest that only a green strategy, which in their study means for the ECB to add green bonds to its balance sheet, contributes to a significant decrease in the stock of pollution if applied during a period of increased QE. Dafermos et al. (2021) come to a similar conclusion but propose to exclude the highly polluting sectors from QE programs. Depending on the need to run and renew asset purchase programs, the ECB should outline her targets of using the taxonomy for certain classes of assets. It may also be desirable to apply a "green twist" to its balance sheet: the ECB would phase out its private-issued bonds in exchange for long-term green bonds issued by the EIB (New Economics Foundation et al. 2020, p. 6). Another potentially more promising tool from the list of unconventional monetary policy measures is to employ targeted and longer-term refinancing operations (TLTROs). By tying central bank lending to the extension of loans to the real sector, they realize an economic stabilization function which could come in handy for meeting greening objectives. Boer and van't Klooster (2021) suggest that the program could start of by targeting certain sectors, such as the construction sector, and continue to support existing legislation such as the Green Deal and the European Recovery Program.

Prong III: Creating and Supporting New Instruments for Green Fiscal Policy
The relationship between fiscal and monetary policies is an issue that has received a huge amount of renewed attention in recent years. After several decades of monetary dominance, in which macroeconomic management has been based on the fiction that monetary policy can be conceived as a stabilization tool not much related to fiscal policy, multiple financial and other crises have highlighted the relationship between the monetary and the fiscal. A study by the Bank for International Settlements supports this assertion by showing how the pandemic has increased the use of unconventional monetary policies worldwide and that the line to the fiscal terrain gets increasingly blurred (Cantú et al. 2021). The academic discussion on this relationship is by no means completed. Some, like most proponents of Modern Monetary Theory, deny that a conceptual difference should be upheld at all and that a separation of the two spheres is futile. Others hope that technological changes might lead to private moneys without any fiscal dimension. In between these extremes, the debate focuses on suitable arrangements to coordinate the two spheres (Reichlin and Schoenmaker 2020) and the question whether and how, in normal times and during crises, central banks should support fiscal policy more explicitly.

We do not weigh in on these debates. Rather, we suggest that the current environment makes it highly unlikely that central banks will not need to support fiscal policy and work together with fiscal policymakers in a coordinated manner. Even fiscally strong countries with a high degree of monetary sovereignty are currently facing the challenge to deal with multiple crises in a time in which the future path for interest rates is highly uncertain. Fiscally weaker countries might well need a continued and strong commitment of the ECB to act as lender of last resort, one that is not impaired by the constant threat of judicial intervention. On top of this and even more relevant for the purpose of this paper, the need for public investment to tackle climate change and other environmental problems is both unprecedentedly large and of a very short-term nature. Most of the needed investment will have to be upfront and carried out in the next 10 years.

Against this backdrop, the ECB needs a clear framework for its role in fiscal policy during the transformation. In this framework, the potential need to support the transition to climate neutrality and environmental sustainability through money creation should be explicitly recognized. Moreover, there should be a formal acknowledgment that the ECB can and should act as a lender of last resort for national governments and the EU, which, through the Green Deal and COVID measures, is increasingly becoming a separate fiscal entity. Within such a framework, the ECB would be enabled to draw upon its capacity to make direct transfers to households and to monetize public debt spent on measures to tackle the ecological crisis. Such measures would need to be backed up by governance arrangements that ensure democratic control and legitimacy, close coordination between the different fiscal agents, and a commitment to preserve the ECB's financial independence through risk-sharing arrangements.

What would this imply more concretely? In many ways, our proposal resembles the one in Couppey-Soubeyran and Delandre (2021). However, we would not share the view that one should strive for a completely "new mode of money issuance."

Rather, we would prefer formalizing the ability of the ECB to support fiscal policy, specifically in the context of the green transformation. First, one would explicitly allow the ECB to take into account the fiscal implications of its monetary policy, for example, in the context of specifying secondary objectives. Second, the ability to act as lender of last resort would be sanctioned through a legal act. Finally, some form of explicit monetary financing ("helicopter money") should be allowed under clearly specified circumstances. Among the different options available for such financing (see, for example, Belke, 2018), the one most suitable for the purpose of the needed socioeconomic transformation would be some form of central bank-financed public investment or tax cuts that compensate the burden of high environmental levies. All this would require setting up a separate and formalized body to coordinate respective policies and establishing parliamentary institutions to steer and control them. Moreover, a formal rule for risk-sharing would need to be established, which specifies in detail who bears the costs of the measures. It is worth noting that these measures would, in contrast to many of our other proposals, require a change of the Treaties, establishing the EU as a fully legitimized fiscal entity.

4 Conclusion

Based on a critique of the recent strategy review, we set out a draft agenda for the ECB that would enable it to fulfill a transformative role in the current ecological and socioeconomic emergency. Moreover, we provide a set of ideas on how legislative bodies on the European level can adequately respond to the exceptional challenges ahead, by "democratically embedding central banking" (Dezernat Zukunft 2020). Our aim was to first highlight how central banking, in its public-private shape, acts like a magnifying glass for socioeconomic transformations that have taken and are taking place and that in order to discuss their constitution and strategy, this perspective needs to be taken into account. Secondly, we wanted to bring together two strands of literature, one on the greening of central bank operations and the other on improving its governance, to point out concrete possibilities of central bank reform which are informed by history and the workings of money as a malleable institution.

We showed that the long-standing view that central banks originated from private financial networks and should have a large enough distance to the public sector needs to be challenged, both on the grounds of more recent historical accounts of central banking and on the ground of current necessities. Due to the exigencies of planetary boundaries and due to the evidently greater political role they have taken on in the past decades, the question of how to re-embed the central bank as a democratically legitimized state institution needs to be answered promptly. We provided an overview of the historical changes in their embeddedness, in Polanyian terms. The special danger a central bank runs in modern times is that pressures to provide excessive monetary expansion can originate from different groups or classes. This means that concerns about an overexpansion of money have to be taken seriously. But rather than implying that these expansions originate from the institutions of (social) democracy, the historical record shows that embedding the central bank in robust democratic institutions helps rather than endangers good policy over the longer term. It might lead to a little more inflation but stabilizes the political economy in a more fundamental sense. This implies that more democratic control over central banks would not only be justified, but expedient, especially under the conditions of an ecological emergency. In resemblance to the New Deal and the Bretton Woods regime, the EU Green Deal and recovery programs such as Next Generation EU might provide an opportunity to map out a more active role of the central bank as a state institution. EU lawmakers and other political actors seem to be increasingly aware of that but may lack the instruments and the ideological neutrality to transcend the neo-liberal origins of the current set-up. A paradigm shift seems to be ongoing, but the language of neoliberalism has not yet been unlearned.

The result of such an ongoing paradigm shift in central banking, with sticky past ideologies and contours of new ones, is reflected in the ECB strategy review which was published in July 2021. While acknowledging the ubiquity of ecological factors, it sticks to a tight frame of inflation targeting and forwent the opportunity to establish the secondary mandate as an anchor for political checks and balances. The displacement of an ecological agenda to the sphere of measurement and indicators leaves the direction of travel of the ECB with regard to combating further multilayered crises unclear. We argue, as others have done, that the strategy will not only cause higher economic costs, as the ECB policies will continue to operate in a mismatch with its political foundations. It will almost certainly prevent a more effective reduction of ecological instability as much as social inequality and thereby fail to solve the problems it is ought to address alongside legislative bodies. This, then, would be a bane rather than a boost for ECB credibility.

By focusing on monetary policy, contextualizing institutions and strategies, and taking into account current challenges, we have formulated a proposal that we believe to be both bold enough (to really make a difference in terms of the European and global efforts to tackle climate change) and democratically legitimized (by taking into account issues of accountability and governance). Most importantly, this requires recognizing the political nature of both climate change and central banking. As a consequence, we do neither deny the need for a reasonable amount of central bank independence, not do we fall into the trap to making it an absolute principle that stands in the way of reasonable policies. Instead, we believe our proposal is principle-based, as it emphasizes the need for (1) democratic legitimacy, political control, and accountability; (2) policy, operational, and financial independence; and (3) a bold, quick, and coordinated response of EU institutions to the pressing problem of climate change.

Acknowledgments We would like to thank the Federal Ministry for Education and Science (BMBF) for generous research support in the context of its program on "Sustainable Finance and Climate Protection"/"Klimaschutz und Finanzwirtschaft" (KlimFi). For helpful comments and discussion, we would like to thank Bernhard Emunds, Friedhelm Hengsbach, Gerhard Illing, Marvin Drach, Moritz Hütten, Nele Braun, Ndidi Nnoli-Edozien, Richmond Boakye, and Sonja

Kleinod. We are also thankful for suggestions from participants of the research seminar of ZNWU/SECP (W:NE), at a research workshop of the Nell-Breuning Institute at University Saint George, Frankfurt, and at the conference "The State in the Great Transformation" at the Protestant Academy in Tutzing, organized by the Yearbook "Institutional and Normative Foundations of Economics." We are appreciative to the SECP team for research support.

Appendix

Table 1 Proposals to green ECB instruments and operations

Proposal	Main instruments discussed	Main policy approach	Quotes
Couppey-Soubeyran (2020)	MROs, collateral, TLTROs, or QE, public asset purchases, green helicopter money	• Objective of environmental sustainability should be included in the ECB's mandate • Gradually move from "light green" (MROs, collateral, TLTROs, or QE) to "brighter light green" (public asset purchases) to bright green. • Adjust institutional set-up accordingly	"It is not up to the central bank to define the route to ecological transition. Neither is it up to States alone, since the coordination needed for the ecological transition will involve new institutional structures to enable joint decisions to be taken by all stakeholders: States, central banks, NGOs, scientists and civil society. Institutional changes will be necessary and the independence of central banks will undoubtedly be called into question." "In order to move towards the 'bright green' option, it will probably be necessary to pass through the shades of 'light green' first, less for substantive reasons than due to the institutional and political blockages that are not easy to dislodge. As such, this note presents 'small steps' within a constant institutional framework"
Dafermos et al. (2021).	Collateral framework	• Adjust the collateral list alongside a climate-aligned haircut framework • Rewrite eligibility	"...even an aggressive calibration of haircuts to reflect the relative greenness/dirtiness of collateral will not

(continued)

Table 1 (continued)

Proposal	Main instruments discussed	Main policy approach	Quotes
		criteria and replace dirty bonds with greener bonds, including those issued by carbon-intensive companies. • Do take into account incentives of carbon-intensive industries and funding needs of financial and real sector entities	reduce significantly the carbon intensity of the ECB's collateral list." "...for the ECB to seriously tackle the carbon bias hardwired into its collateral rules, it needs to adjust the collateral list alongside a climate-aligned haircut framework. The ECB has to rewrite eligibility criteria and replace dirty bonds with greener bonds, including those issued by carbon-intensive companies." "Critically, even our more climate-friendly scenario does not eliminate carbon-intensive companies from the list of eligible issuers.... This encourages companies to accelerate the transition to low-carbon activities." "These scenarios preserve banks' access to central bank money..."
Jourdan and Kalinowski (2019)	Green QE	• Reinvest revenues from programs such as the CSPP	"This policy note suggests a way to integrate carbon emissions as a criterion in its own right, shaping central banks' investment decisions and the collateral framework used for refinancing purposes. As the ECB intends to maintain its balance sheet volume at its current level even after the Quantitative Easing officially ends, the most urgent decisions concern the reinvestment of revenues from programs such as the CSPP. We consider that the

(continued)

Table 1 (continued)

Proposal	Main instruments discussed	Main policy approach	Quotes
			technical difficulties related to estimating carbon emissions for different financial assets are real but surmountable and should not justify inaction."
New Economics Foundation and Positive Money (2020)	All existing and new ones, including Green TLTROs (targeted longer-term refinancing operations)	• Take a holistic approach • Coordinate with other public players, in particular EIB • Lead by example	"The ECB must: 1. Align its asset purchasing programmes and collateral frameworks with the Paris Climate Agreement, to support the low carbon transition. 2. Align its refinancing operations to the banking sector with the Paris Agreement to encourage more sustainable bank lending and fill the green investment gap. 3. Support asset markets for sustainable investment and coordinate operations with the European Investment Bank (or other equivalent European institutions) to ramp up green investment and lock-in a low carbon future. 4. Implement prudential measures to increase the resilience of the European banking sector to climate risks and reduce brown financial flows (e.g. financing of fossil fuels). 5. Lead by example on climate disclosures and transparency by assessing and regularly communicating to elected officials the alignment of its operations with the Paris Agreement and that of the European banking sector."

(continued)

Table 1 (continued)

Proposal	Main instruments discussed	Main policy approach	Quotes
Oustry et al. (2020)	Collateral framework	• Focus on climate-related financial risks, aim for aggregate alignment of collateral pool with climate targets • Take into account limits of asset-by-asset approach • Recognize that ECB is already exposed to climate risk, but preserve "market neutrality" and "residual risk equivalence"	"Generally speaking, applied to a central bank's collateral policy, this approach would entail: 1. Identifying and selecting existing 'alignment' methodologies and metrics that capture the extent to which assets and issuers contribute to meeting the Paris Agreement's target limit of 2°C (or 1.5°C); 2. Considering the collateral a counterparty pledges to participate in liquidity providing operations as a portfolio of assets; and 3. Measuring and monitoring its 'temperature' over time by reference to a benchmark value." "The numerical experiment using Eurosystem marketable criteria data suggests that, in aggregate, neither the Eurosystem eligible collateral universe nor the collateral pledged is 'aligned' with the climate targets of the European Union"
Schnabel (2021)	Collateral framework and QE	• Move from market neutrality to market efficiency, recognizing that a supposedly "neutral" market allocation may be suboptimal in the presence of externalities • Consider a wide spectrum of instruments (including asset purchases, broadening or constraining collateral framework) and supervisory stress tests	"There is a wide spectrum of other possible avenues that the ECB and other central banks could pursue to contribute to the global fight against climate change. [. . .] Any climate change policy hinges on the availability of **reliable data**." ". . . We could amend our **collateral framework**, for example by

(continued)

Table 1 (continued)

Proposal	Main instruments discussed	Main policy approach	Quotes
		• Take into account alternative implementation strategies, including tilting • Tendency to adopt a more data-driven gradualism	including innovative financial products as eligible collateral, as we have recently done with the acceptance of sustainability-linked bonds, or by linking the eligibility as collateral to more comprehensive disclosures. . ." "In greening its asset portfolio, the ECB could pursue several alternative strategies. Some have argued that we should implement outright exclusion policies—also known as negative screening policies—by stopping purchases of bonds issued by polluting sectors. . . . Such policies have the drawback that they would eliminate incentives for firms in carbon-intensive sectors to reduce their greenhouse gas emissions." "However, the consequences of any potential policy initiatives need to be thoroughly evaluated against the limitations stipulated by the Treaties. Our measures must always remain without prejudice to our primary mandate of safeguarding price stability."
Schoenmaker (2019)	Green QE/collateral base	• Tilt asset and collateral base for monetary policy operations toward low-carbon assets • Recognize that portfolio is currently overweight in high carbon companies.	"Central banks have a long-term perspective (often making reference to sustainable economic growth) and are therefore mindful of the impact of climate change on stability. They have already

(continued)

Table 1 (continued)

Proposal	Main instruments discussed	Main policy approach	Quotes
		• Take a modest approach at first	started to examine the impact of climate change on the stability of the financial system from a risk management perspective. On the monetary side, there is no comparable direct impact on price stability, which has a medium-term horizon." "The Eurosystem could support the EU's climate policy by greening monetary policy operations. The basic idea would be to tilt the asset and collateral base for these operations towards low-carbon assets."
UNEP (2017)	Green QE + Regulation	• Use menu of greening options, including regulation and QE • Take a green asset management approach • Take into account need for institutional reform	"At a more general level, central banks could manage their assets according to social impact investment standards." "While making the case for a pro-active, 'sustainable development role of central banks, the paper also discusses the risks of overstretching central banks' mandates and vesting too much power in unaccountable institutions as well as the division of labor between central banks and other institutions."
van't Klooster and van Tilburg (2020)	Green TLTROs (targeted longer-term refinancing operations)	• Provide cheap funding if banks lend in accordance with EU taxonomy of green activities • Use this as entry point to a more general greening • Take into account side effects of other (banking	"Green TLTROs will contribute to achieving the ECB's primary mandate by addressing market failures that undermine the broader economic preconditions of monetary stability;" "Green TLTROs will

(continued)

Table 1 (continued)

Proposal	Main instruments discussed	Main policy approach	Quotes
		regulation, collateral framework, QE)	support the ECB's efforts to reduce environmental and climate-related financial risk built up in banks' balance sheets and thereby contribute to financial stability;" "Green TLTROs will help to align monetary policy with the ECB's secondary mandate, which requires it to support the EU's environmental objectives where this is possible without prejudice to price stability."
Weidmann (2021)	Collateral framework and QE	• Focus on climate-related financial risks and enhancing transparency • Proceed slowly • Refrain from making adjustments due to climate policy considerations	"That is why I have recommended that, in future, the Eurosystem should only purchase securities or accept them as collateral if their issuers meet certain climate-related reporting obligations" "In the end, these two measures could change the composition of our monetary policy portfolios—always under the premise that those bond holdings are needed for price stability. But the measures cannot be introduced immediately: issuers need time to provide the necessary information..." "If no adequate solution can be found here, the Eurosystem would have to adopt alternative measures to properly incorporate climate-related financial risks into its risk management, for example by

(continued)

Table 1 (continued)

Proposal	Main instruments discussed	Main policy approach	Quotes
			limiting the maturities or the amount of corporate bonds of certain sectors and issuers in the Eurosystem's monetary policy portfolio. Such risk-oriented tilting should not be confused with suggestions to steer the behavior of companies and financial institutions for political reasons."

Table 2 Proposals for institutional change

Policy field	Paper	Main policy takeaway
Mandate interpretation	Markus Demary & Michael Hüther, 9. Dezember 2020. ECB Strategy Review - The New Pillars: Communication and Climate Change	We advise the ECB to strengthen its communication especially with social groups unfamiliar with monetary policy. When it comes to climate change, the **ECB should be responsive, but not activist**. The Fed switched to average inflation targeting. As a consequence, the strategy change to average inflation targeting **could be interpreted as a justification for a longer period of expansionary monetary policy by the broader public**. Climate risks are becoming increasingly relevant for the financial sector. The **rating agencies** are taking climate risks into account in their ratings and, increasingly, rating downgrades due to weather risks are taking place instead. If climate risks cause the **creditworthiness** of companies to fall and thus credit risks to rise, the ECB must **address this in its collateral framework**. In this way, the ECB is quite capable of accompanying the general trend toward sustainable finance; **it must even do so in its role as supervisor** (if, for example, credit risks from green projects are underestimated). Moreover, a change in investment

(continued)

Table 2 (continued)

Policy field	Paper	Main policy takeaway
		behavior can influence the transmission process, which would be relevant for the ECB. But it can do so from an observing and reacting position. However, it is not the task of a central bank to support or slow down a structural change. That is the task of development banks
Strategy review	Dullien & Tober 2021. ECB Strategy: best practice and new frontiers. IMK Policy Brief No. 105	Proportionality considerations [like in the Weiss case] combined with an overly narrow interpretation of the ECB's mandate would unduly limit the scope of monetary policy. For example, it is possible to justify including climate change considerations in monetary policy decisions with reference to price level stability. However, **arguing that monetary policy should be greener because of the negative impact of climate change on consumption (Lagarde 2020c) is needlessly roundabout** and less intelligible than coherently spelling out the ECB's support of overall EU policies geared toward averting the existential threat of climate change. **Fiscal policy may be more effective than monetary policy in certain circumstances** Monetary and fiscal policy aims will remain intertwined even when economic growth is more vigorous and the inflation target is within reach. Given its responsibilities as laid down in the EU treaty, **the ECB will have to exercise caution in raising rates** and test the limits of inflation-free growth in an effort to reduce unemployment and underemployment, thereby reversing past hysteresis effects. Since EU policymakers have prioritized the reduction in greenhouse gas emissions, the ECB needs to ensure that its policies do not counteract but rather reinforce the EU's climate policies.
Mandate interpretation		The ECB's inflation target, redefined in 2003 as "below but close to two percent," is only marginally less asymmetric and cryptic

(continued)

Table 2 (continued)

Policy field	Paper	Main policy takeaway
		than the initial definition of "below 2%" (ECB 2003, ECB 1998). However, as the strategy evolved over the past 18 years, the inflation target is increasingly interpreted as a symmetric target of 1.9% by the ECB, economists, and others. Within the framework of the ECB's strategy of targeting a specific inflation rate—**after the current review presumably 2%**—in the medium term, **core inflation** serves as an indicator for underlying inflation. The use of core inflation as an important indicator emerged only during Draghi's presidency. One-off price shocks do not require a monetary policy response (Tober/Zimmermann 2009) unless they trigger second-round effects.
Strategy review	ETUC position on the European Central Bank Strategy Review Adopted at the virtual Executive Committee Meeting of 9–10 December 2020	Given the uneven recovery expected in the different Member States—and their difference in public finance management and levels of debts and deficits—a more politicized ECB would be needed, without impairing in any way its independence. A low interest rate policy and active monetary support through **quantitative easing programs and Targeted Long-Term Refinancing Operations (TLTRO)**, for enabling Member States and businesses to access the necessary spending for just ecological transition, increased investment, and quality job creation with strong social standards, could represent a way of exit to the ongoing debates. Full employment and ecological transition objectives to be on a par with price stability in the ECB's mandate; • The ECB **not to tighten monetary policy** just because a decrease in unemployment is in view • The ECB to support, through

(continued)

Table 2 (continued)

Policy field	Paper	Main policy takeaway
		expansionary monetary policies, the increased needs for public investment, through some kind of **yield control** • The ECB to revise its inflation methodology for better **including housing prices developments** • The ECB to consider the possibility of **helicopter money** • The ECB to increase financial regulation as a way to improve monetary transmission mechanisms • The ECB to continue to show willingness to intervene including with unconventional monetary tools in a flexible manner to prevent debt crisis in Europe and allow economic and social upward convergence • The ECB to reorientate its **asset purchase toward bonds issued by companies respecting just ecological transition purposes** • The ECB to: – **Target assets and collaterals in line with the Paris Climate Agreement** and issued by businesses satisfying strong social standards and working rights, to support the low-carbon transition – Make **refinancing operations replacing the old bonds come to maturity with environmental bonds issued by business respectful of good social and work practices, and implement a green and social TLTRO** – Coordinate and support its market operations for sustainable investment **with the European Investment Bank**; Develop a new system of financial regulation based upon asset-based capital requirements for green and social investment – And to lead by example on climate disclosures and transparency by assessing and regularly communicating to elected officials the alignment of its operations with the Paris Agreement and that of the

(continued)

Table 2 (continued)

Policy field	Paper	Main policy takeaway
		European banking sector. We strongly support the role of the European System of Central Banks (ESCB) in providing the public with reliable and detailed data that help to better analyse economic activity. This does not only include of macroeconomic data, data on MFIs, but also data on households as the Household Finance and Consumption Survey (HFCS)
Mandate	Dezernat Zukunft. 2020: 14 ideas for after Corona (DZ)	**ECB's mandate** could be given an automatic 10-year **sunset clause**. Written mandate requires consent from 68 distinct political bodies, among them all EMU member states, so that no gap will be closed if it benefits just one of these bodies
Mandate	Eichengreen, Prasad, Rajan 2011. Rethinking central banking. Vox EU	Financial stability should be an explicit mandate of central banks
Mandate interpretation	De Boer & van t'Klooster 2020. The ECB, the courts and the issue of democratic legitimacy after *Weiss*	The legal mandate of the ECB is broad and contains only a few provisions that provide targeted guidance on how to implement monetary policy (Smits 1997; Gortsos 2020) Article 127 (2) TFEU leaves it to the ECB itself to "**define** and implement the monetary policy of the Union"
Mandate interpretation/primary mandate	DZ	Using an **average inflation target** may increase long-run prosperity without endangering long-term price stability, by preventing premature rates increases like in 2011. Current version, the HICP does not consider the carbon footprint of products. In light of the desirability of higher prices for "brown" consumer goods and services (e.g., petrol, air travel, or meat), **"greening" the HICP** would be one way to take the bite out of the price stability mandate, while at the same time making it more consistent with the ECB's secondary objective DZ A shift from consumer price inflation targeting toward **wage bill flooring** can also be contemplated,

(continued)

Table 2 (continued)

Policy field	Paper	Main policy takeaway
		in line with similar proposals advanced in the US
Mandate interpretation	(Bundesverfassungsgericht)	Climate policy would equal doing economic policy with the help of monetary policy
Secondary objective	DZ	No concerted effort has yet been made to establish clear priorities for the ECB under its **secondary objective**. Spelling out the content of the ECB's secondary objective
Secondary objective	Groepe 2016	Climate could be part of secondary objective, but could result in a situation in which expectations on shift are taken way to high
Operational independence	De Boer & van t'Klooster 2020. The ECB, the courts and the issue of democratic legitimacy after *Weiss*	**Operational targets** and specifications of how they are achieved could be **reviewed on a 5-year schedule**. Such a procedure exists in the United Kingdom where Article 12 of the Bank of England Act 1998 requires that the Treasury spells out the price stability objective and the government's economic policy at least once per year
Accountability	DZ	Euro-Parliament could be created, elected or selected by sortition, either from among the demos at large or from among member state parliamentarians. This parliament, supported by specialist staff to provide expert input, would substitute for the Eurogroup, appoint the ECB governing council, and conduct the 5- and 10-year revisions of the ECB mandate and tool
Accountability	De Boer & van t'Klooster 2020. The ECB, the courts and the issue of democratic legitimacy after *Weiss*	To address how the ECB should deal with the economic policy effects of its operations, the Council can set out broad economic policy guidelines in accordance with the procedure of Article 121 (2) TFEU and articulate how it sees the role of the ECB in realizing its secondary mandate

References

Adloff F, Neckel S (2019) Futures of sustainability as modernization, transformation, and control: a conceptual framework. Sustain Sci 14(4):1015–1025

Alesina A (1988) Macroeconomics and politics. In: NBER macroeconomics annual, vol 3. MIT Press, Cambridge, pp 13–52. https://doi.org/10.1086/654070

Angeloni I (2020) The ECB strategy review. Walking a narrow path. https://cepr.org/voxeu/blogs-and-reviews/ecb-strategy-review-walking-narrow-path

Battilossi S, Cassis Y, Yago K (eds) (2020) Handbook of the history of money and currency. Springer Singapore, Singapore

Belke A (2018) Helicopter money: should Central Banks rain money from the sky? Intereconomics 2018(1):34–40. https://www.intereconomics.eu/con-tents/year/2018/number/1/article/helicopter-money-should-central-banks-rain-money-from-the-sky.html

Bindseil U (2019) Central banking before 1800. A rehabilitation, 1st edn. Oxford University Press, Oxford

Blanchard O, Dell'Ariccia G, Mauro P (2010) Rethinking macroeconomic policy. J Money Credit Bank 42(1):199–215. https://doi.org/10.1111/j.1538-4616.2010.00334.x

Blot C, et al (2021) A welcome revision rather than a revolution | Think Tank | Parliament Europe. With assistance of Blot, Christophe, Bozou, Caroline and Creel, Jérôme. https://www.europarl.europa.eu/thinktank/mt/document/IPOL_IDA(2021)695475. Accessed 30 Mar 2022

Boltanski L, Thévenot L (2018) Über die Rechtfertigung. Eine Soziologie der kritischen Urteilskraft, 2. Aufl. Hamburger Edition, Hamburg

Burawoy M (2012) Manufacturing consent. University of Chicago Press, Chicago

Canepa F, Martin M (2020) ECB's Lagarde launches policy overhaul that will leave no stone unturned. Reuters. https://www.reuters.com/article/us-ecb-policy-idUSKBN1ZL32Y. Accessed Mar 2022

Cantú C, Cavallino P, Fiore FD, Yetman J (2021) A global database on Central Banks' monetary responses to Covid-19. BIS Working Papers No 934

Chang M, Hodson D (2019) Reforming the European Parliament's monetary and economic dialogues. Creating accountability through a euro area oversight subcommittee. In: Costa O (ed) The European Parliament in times of EU crisis. Dynamics and transformations. Springer (European Administrative Governance), Cham

Claeys G, Domínguez-Jiménez M (2020) How can the European parliament better oversee the European central bank? Study for the committee on economic and monetary affairs, policy department for economic, scientific and quality of life policies, European parliament, Luxembourg

Clar E (2019) The gold standard, deflation and fascism in Polanyi's great transformation. A multidisciplinary analysis (1)

Couppey-Soubeyran J (2020) The role of Monetary Policy in the ecological transition. An overview of various greening options. Veblen Institute for Economic Reforms

Couppey-Soubeyran J, Delandre P (2021) Monetary transition: the case for money serving the common good. Veblen Institute for Economic Reforms. https://www.veblen-institute.org/Monetary-Transition-The-Case-for-Money-serving-the-Common-Good.html. Accessed 30 Mar 2022

Dafermos Y, Gabor D, Nikolaidi M, Pawloff A, van Lerven F (2020) Decarbonising is easy. Beyond market neutrality in the ECB's corporate QE. The New Economics Foundation, London

Dafermos Y, Gabor D, Nikolaidi M, Pawloff A, van Lerven F (2021) Greening the Eurosystem collateral framework. The New Economics Foundation, London

Dale G (2008) Karl Polanyi's The Great transformation: perverse effects, protectionism and Gemeinschaft. Econ Soc 37(4):495–524. https://doi.org/10.1080/03085140802357901

de Boer N, van't Klooster J (2021) The ECB, the courts and the issue of democratic legitimacy after Weiss

Demertzis M, Domínguez-Jiménez M (2020) Monetary policy in the time of COVID-19, or how uncertainty is here to stay. ECON Committee, Brussels

Dezernat Zukunft (2020) 14 ideas for after Corona (DZ). https://dezernatzukunft.org/
Diaz-Bone R (2015) Die "Économie des conventions". Grundlagen und Entwicklungen der neuen französischen Wirtschaftssoziologie, 1. Aufl. Springer VS, Wiesbaden. http://search.ebscohost.com/login.aspx?direct=true & scope=site & db=nlebk & AN=966907.
Dornbusch R, Favero C, Giavazzi F (1998) Immediate challenges for the European Central Bank. 13(26):16–64
Dullien S, Tober S (2021) ECB strategy. Best practice and new frontiers. IMK policy brief no. 105. Macroeconomic Policy Institute (IMK) of Hans-Böckler-Foundation, Düsseldorf.
ECB (2021a) The ECB's monetary policy strategy statement 2021a. https://www.ecb.europa.eu/home/search/review/html/ecb.strategyreview_monpol_strategy_statement.en.html
ECB (2021b) An overview of the ECB's monetary policy strategy 2021b. https://www.ecb.europa.eu/home/search/review/html/ecb.strategyreview_monpol_strategy_statement.en.html
Epstein G (2013) Developmental central banking: winning the future by updating a page from the past. Review of Keynesian Economics 1(3):273–287. https://doi.org/10.4337/roke.2013.03.02
Ferrari A, Landi V (2020) Whatever it takes to save the planet? Central banks and unconventional green policy. European Central Bank, Frankfurt am Main (ECB Working paper series, no 2500, December 2020)
Goodhart C (1985) The evolution of central banks, 3rd edn. MIT Press, Cambridge, MA
Hauser A (2021, May 21) It's not easy being green – but that shouldn't stop us: how central banks can use their monetary policy portfolio to support orderly transition to net zero. Bank of England - Speech. London
Hütten M, Klüh U (2017) No more Cakes and Ale: banks and banking regulation in the post-Bretton Woods macro-regime. In: Heinemann F, Klüh U, Watzka S (eds) Monetary policy, financial crises, and the macroeconomy. Festschrift for Gerhard Illing. With assistance of Gerhard Illing, 1st edn. Springer, Cham, pp 325–349
Issing O (2019) What operating procedures should be adopted to maintain price stability? Practical issues (commentary), pp 287–296
Kern A, Lastra R M (2020) The ECB mandate: perspectives on sustainability and solidarity Policy Department for Economic, Scientific and Quality of Life Policies Directorate-General for Internal Policies: European Parliament. https://www.europarl.europa.eu/thinktank/en/document/IPOL_IDA(2020)648813
Klüh U (2015) Denken in Makroregimes und Große Transformationen. Eine Anwenderperspektive. Jahbruch normative und institutionelle Grundfragen der Ökonomik 14:135–164
Klüh U (2021) Public management: Ertüchtigte Staatlichkeit vor dem Hintergrund des poli-tischen Paradoxons. Hochschule Darmstadt, Fachbereich Wirtschaft, Zentrum für Nachhaltige Wirtschafts- und Unternehmenspolitik ZNWU (ZNWU Discussion Paper, 6), Darmstadt. https://www.econstor.eu/handle/10419/235474
Land R (2019a) Ökokapital: Bedingungen der Möglichkeit eines neuen Regimes wirt-schaftlicher Entwicklung; ein systemtheoretischer Bauplan 12, p 204. https://www.ssoar.info/ssoar/bitstream/document/67299/1/ssoar-2019-land-Okokapital_Bedingungen_der_Moglichkeit_eines.pdf
Land R (2019b) Ökokapital: Bedingungen der Möglichkeit eines neuen Regimes wirtschaftlicher Entwicklung; ein systemtheoretischer Bauplan. Forschungsinstitut für gesellschaft-liche Weiterentwicklung e.V. (FGW), Düsseldorf
Lehndorff S (2020) New Deal heißt Mut zum Konflikt. Was wir von Roosevelts Reform-politik der 1930er Jahre heute lernen können: eine Flugschrift. VSA Verlag, Hamburg
Mader P, Mertens D, van der Zwan N (eds) (2020) The Routledge international handbook of financialization, 1st edn. Routledge, New York
Marsh D (1992) Die Bundesbank. Geschäfte mit der Macht, 1. Aufl. Bertelsmann, Gütersloh
Mertens D, Thiemann M (2019) Building a hidden investment state? The European investment bank, national development banks and European economic governance. J Eur Public Policy 26(1):23–43. https://doi.org/10.1080/13501763.2017.1382556
Murau S (2020) A Macro-Financial Model of the Eurozone Architecture Embedded in the Global Offshore US-Dollar System. Global Economic Governance Initiative

Needham DJ (2020) The evolution of Monetary policy (goals and targets) in western Europe. In: Handbook of the history of money and currency. Springer Singapore, Singapore, pp 857–882

Neumann FL (ed) (1942 [2018]): Behemoth. Struktur und Praxis des Nationalsozialismus 1933-1944. Ungekürzte Ausg., 5. Aufl. CEP Europäische Verlagsanstalt (Fischer-Taschenbücher Die Zeit des Nationalsozialismus, 4306), Hamburg

New Economics Foundation; Positive Money; 350 (2020) The ECB and climate change: outlining a vision for success. New Economics Foundation, Positive Money, 350. London

Oustry A, Erkan B, Svartzman R, Weber PF (2020) Climate-related risks and central banks' collateral policy: a methodological experiment. Revue economique 73(2):173–218

Paniagua P (2021) The institutional evolution of Central Banks

Pettifor A (2019) The case for the green new deal. Verso, London

Pixley J (2018) Central banks, democratic states and financial power. Cambridge University Press, Cambridge

Polanyi K (1944 [2001]) The great transformation: the political and economic origins of our time. Beacon Press, Bosto

Posen A (ed) (1995) NBER macroeconomics annual. With assistance of Ben S. Bernanke, Julio Rotemberg. National Bureau of Economic Research, MIT Press, Cambridge, MA. http://www.nber.org/chapters/c11021

Posen A (2010, June 14) When Central Banks buy bonds. Independence and the power to say no. New York

Reichlin L, Schoenmaker D (2020) Fault lines in fiscal-monetary policy coordination. https://voxeu.org/article/fault-lines-fiscal-monetary-policy-coordination.

Reichlin L, Adam K, Mckibbin W, McMahon M, Reis R, Ricco G, Weder di Mauro B (2021) The ECB strategy: the 2021 review and its future. https://cepr.org/publications/books-and-reports/ecb-strategy-2021-review-and-its-future

Savevska M (2019) The fictitious commodification of money and the Euro experiment. Pract Eur Cult 4(1)

Schnabel I (2021, June 14) From market neutrality to market efficiency. ECB DG-Research Symposium "Climate change, financial markets and green growth". ECB, Frankfurt am Main

Schnabel I (2022) A new age of energy inflation: climateflation, fossilflation and greenflation. https://www.ecb.eu-ropa.eu/press/key/date/2022/html/ecb.sp220317_2~dbb3582f0a.en.html

Schoenmaker D (2021) Greening monetary policy. Clim Policy 21(4):581–592. https://doi.org/10.1080/14693062.2020.1868392

Smith VC, Yeager LB (1990) The rationale of central banking and the free banking alternative. Reprinted. Liberty Fund and Liberty Press Ed, Indianapolis

Stiglitz JE (2001) Foreword. In: Polanyi K (ed) The great transformation: the political and economic origins of our time. Beacon Press, Boston

Sturn R, Hirschbrunn K, Klüh U (eds) (2019) Kapitalismus und Freiheit. Metropolis-Verlag für Ökonomie Gesellschaft und Politik GmbH. Metropolis-Verlag (Jahrbuch Normative und institutionelle Grundfragen der Ökonomik, Jahrbuch 17), Marburg

Ugolini S (2017) The evolution of Central Banking. Palgrave Macmillan Limited (Palgrave Studies in Economic History Series), London. https://ebookcen-tral.proquest.com/lib/gbv/detail.action?docID=5153531

Ugolini S (2020) The historical evolution of Central Banking. In: Handbook of the history of money and currency. Springer Singapore, Singapore, pp 835–856

Credibility in the Financial Market: A Practical Perspective

von Jens Minnemann

Abstracts The following article presents the view of a practicing financial service provider. The author is the founder of Vision for Finance GmbH, a strategy consulting company whose core mission is to accompany and advise wealthy private individuals, companies, church institutions, and foundations.

1 Introduction: Credibility Is Priceless

Credibility is the key to long-term, sustainable, stable, and economically successful relationships based on partnership. This is especially true in the financial markets. The granting of credit to third parties has always been linked to their credibility. It is not without reason that the term "credit" has its roots in the Latin *credere*, i.e., to believe in, to confide, to hold to be true, and to trust in (Glare 2012).

Can I trust my counterpart is the key question – both for providers of financial services with regard to their clients and for clients with regard to their financial service providers. Without mutual trust, there would be no financial market at all. Our current financial system only works if the actors involved can trust each other. Trust requires credibility (on the relationship between trust and credibility, see also Lis and Korchmar 2013b, p. 22). Credibility is "in a sense a precursor to trust" (Reinmuth 2009, p. 132). In this respect, credibility of the acting persons is the essential key for a functioning financial system.

> Credibility is a leader's currency. With it, he or she is solvent; without it, he or she is bankrupt. (John C. Maxwell (+1947), US-American author, speaker, and coach in Maxwell 2009)

This article examines the question of what credibility is and how the credibility of a financial service provider can be recognized. The credibility of the financial services sector is examined and illustrated with a number of practical examples.

von Jens Minnemann (✉)
Veitshöchheim, Germany
e-mail: jm@visionforfinance.com

H. J. Bolsinger et al. (eds.), *The European Central Bank and Its Role in a Sustainable Finance System*, Sustainable Finance, https://doi.org/10.1007/978-3-031-24478-0_5

2 About Credibility

Based on the thesis expressed in the introduction that "credibility of the acting persons is the essential key for a functioning financial system," it is surprising that the term credibility is largely undefined especially in the German-language literature. Thus, Nawratil (Nawratil 1997) notes:

> "Formal definitions are thin on the ground; even scientific studies usually move straight to operationalisation without providing an exact clarification of terms" (Nawratil 1997, p. 15) and also (Lis and Korchmar 2013b) conclude in their research that "a uniform definition of credibility . . . has not yet been established" (Lis and Korchmar 2013b, p. 21). Nevertheless, there are numerous approaches to defining credibility.

Thus, an etymological derivation by Gössmann leads to the conclusion that credibility is directed both at persons and at their statements. "In the 15th century it [the word credible] first appears in the language of legal life and gradually displaces the word 'glaubhaft', which comes from Middle High German and means something like trustworthy. It is therefore first used of persons in the sense that they can be trusted with regard to their truthfulness and reliability. In addition, it is also used of statements, testimonies, news, calculations, because they seem to correspond to the truth without objective proof being possible" (Wilhelm Gössmann: Glaubwürdigkeit im Sprachgebrauch. Stilkritische und sprachdidaktische Untersuchungen, Munich 1970, p. 23. quoted after Nawratil 1997). Bentele follows a similar idea in his definition of credibility: "Credibility can be defined as a property attributed to people, institutions or their communicative products (oral or written texts, audio-visual representations). Credibility is thus not understood here as an inherent property of texts, but as an element of at least a four-digit relation. Credibility of a person (or institution) X is given when at least two conditions are met: (a) the communication partner (or recipient) Y must be able to trust that the statements x1-n about the events z1-n are true, that they adequately describe z1-n; (b) the communicative behaviour of X must show a minimum of coherence, it must be 'coherent'. This trust is established through repeated positive experiences or is constituted and supported by characteristics such as social status, expertness, independence from partial interests, etc." (Günter Bentele: The Factor Credibility. Research results and questions for the socialisation perspective, in: Publizistik 33/1988, pp. 406–426, 408 quoted after (Nawratil 1997, p. 16)). According to Bentele, credibility is the result of an attribution process in which the receiver trusts the truth of the sender's statement because the sender is characterized by coherent communication behavior. Credibility is thus not an inherent property of texts, but arises through attribution (Lis and Korchmar 2013b, p. 21). The quintessence here is the veracity of the information ((Lis and Korchmar 2013b, p. 22). According to the research conducted by the Yale group around Hovland and Weiss (1951), credibility is a two-dimensional construct. Expertness and trustworthiness are the foundations of credibility.

Research on credibility in subsequent decades has produced numerous other factors, some of which differ significantly, such as "believability, trust, reliability, accuracy, fairness, objectivity, etc." (Hilligos and Rieh 2008, p. 1468 cited in (Lis and Korchmar 2013a, p. 22)). Eisend (2003) adds the function of substituting missing objective evidence to the previous definitions: "Credibility is a multidimensional concept for the assessment of a communication source by the recipient of information. This assessment is based on subjective perception and is context specific. Credibility substitutes for missing objective evidence and therefore represents an information surrogate that determines the recipient's degree of willingness to adopt the information received from the source as cognition into the self, attributing to it a certain content in terms of correspondence with reality" (Eisend 2003, p. 64). Credibility is not a permanent condition, but "must be acquired in an ongoing process" (Thommen 2003, p. 47). Thommen develops a simplified but practical definition of credibility: "Being credible means nothing more than that one considers the company worthy of assuming a function in society. It is believed and trusted in terms of what it says or does" (Thommen 2003, p. 45). For the following consideration of the credibility of a financial service provider, this working definition is used:

> Credibility is the attribute imputed to a person or institution that their statements are true without the presentation of objective evidence.

Credibility means that I do what I say and that I thereby become assessable and reliable in the perception of my counterpart. This reliability makes relationships sustainable, lasting, and resilient. Credibility is thus the key to long-term relationships based on partnership. This also applies to business relationships, such as that between company and customer. This is especially true in the financial sector. The value of a currency or the value of money depends on the credibility of a central bank or government to accept the currency as a means of exchange and payment. The preservation and increase of an investor's wealth depends on whether he can trust the statements of his bank or his asset manager and whether these do what they say. Credibility is therefore – for financial service providers and their clients – priceless.

3 What Is the Credibility of a Financial Service Provider?

The finding that no uniform definition of credibility has yet developed in the literature has the consequence that there are also no uniformly related criteria for measuring or verifying credibility. "Despite the large number of studies, there is a lack of clear and systematic criteria for operationalising the two dimensions of 'competence' and 'trustworthiness'" (Nawratil 1997, p. 54). Credibility research deals with the question of which determinants influence the emergence or attribution of credibility. Three different approaches to the assessment of credibility have developed: the behavior-oriented, the content-oriented, and the source- or context-oriented approach (Nawratil 1997, p. 25; Eisend 2003, p. 94).

For the study of credibility in the financial market, the source- and context-oriented approach is helpful due to its high relevance. It examines "which behavior-independent characteristics of a source lead to its credibility being attributed to it" (Nawratil 1997, p. 218). Sources can be the communicator as well as the message itself.

In the literature, the credibility of the communicator ("source credibility") is the focus of numerous studies. The starting point is often the "source credibility theory" (Hovland et al. 1953). This theory bases the analysis of the communicator's credibility on the factor's expertise (expertness) and trustworthiness. The 20th Edelman Trust Barometer from 2019 (Lübbert 2020) concludes that "competence and ethics are the two most important criteria that drive people to institutional trust in companies" (Bolsinger 2022).

In the following, the author describes five characteristics from his own consultancy practice by means of which the credibility of a financial service provider, as a communicator, can be examined and evaluated (operationalized). He uses the central factors of "expertness" and "trustworthiness" and adds the characteristic of "fairness." In addition to these three characteristics, there are many other features, such as similarity, dynamics, etc. (Giffin 1967; Simons et al. cited in Lis and Korchmar (2013b, p. 26)) to assess credibility.

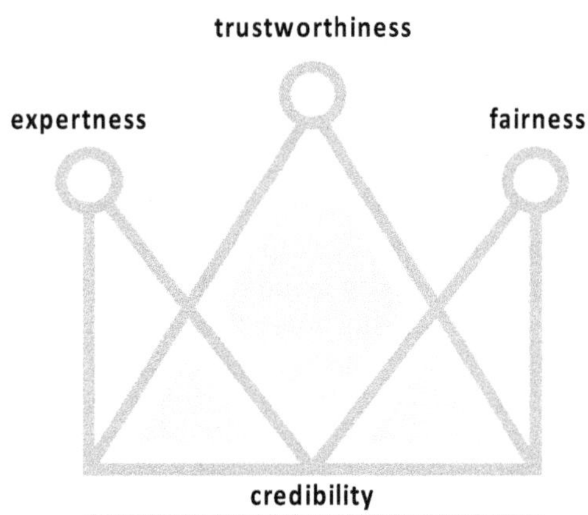

"Credibility Crown" After Jens Minnemann

3.1 *Focus on Core Mission and Core Competence (Expertness)*

A financial services company (communicator) is credible when it focuses on its core competence and mission.

A company's core competence is its most essential capability. As a rule, it is the core competence that leads to a company performing better than its competitors, thereby creating a competitive advantage and consequently growing the company.

The focus on the core competencies leads, as expected, to the company consistently providing excellent services in these performance areas. The customer (recipient) can rely on the fact that the quality of the service is high. This leads – with fair prices (see Point 3: "Alignment of the Range of Services with the Needs of the Customer") – to high customer satisfaction, and this in turn leads to the company being perceived and classified as credible by its customers.

For this to succeed, it is first necessary to clarify what the core mission and core competences of the company are. This requires knowing one's own competences, being able to evaluate them objectively, and assessing which skills are only average or even below average. Following Jay Barnes' (Barney and Hesterly 2015) VRIO method, the following questions can be asked to identify core competencies:

- What skills (competences, knowledge, etc.) does the company have?
- Which competences give the company a competitive advantage?
- Can these competences be imitated by third parties?
- Can the company exploit the existing competences?

To achieve the best possible results, it is advisable to involve the company's stakeholders – especially the company's customers – when answering these questions. Furthermore, the answers should be recorded in writing. This makes them visible, verifiable, and communicable. This visibility ("transparency") is an important step on the way to gaining credibility and building trust (DiPiazza and Eccles 2002). In this way, the financial service provider makes it clear to its customers in which service areas it has its core competencies and thus provides excellent services for its customers.

Clients, on the other hand, are advised to ask their financial service providers specific questions about their core competencies (see also Point 2: "Honest and Clear Communication of the Service Offer") and to find out in which services excellent results are not achieved. The combination of expertise presented by the company and "verified" by the customer creates credibility in favor of the company.

3.2 *Honest and Clear Communication of the Service Offer (Trustworthiness)*

Credible financial service providers communicate their range of services honestly, comprehensibly, and in a comprehensive manner.

Honest means presenting the range of services in a way that reflects reality. This includes highlighting strengths and not concealing weaknesses. Comprehensible means presenting the range of services in a language that is understandable to the customer, avoiding technical terms as far as possible. Comprehensive means addressing or at least making available all facets of the service offer. Awards, testimonials from customers, reference addresses, certifications, and much more can give a picture of the company's willingness to be subjected to critical scrutiny.

In particular, talking about which service areas a company does not master and accordingly does not offer helps customers to get a precise picture of a company's performance and leads to higher credibility.

3.3 Alignment of the Range of Services with the Needs of the Customer (Expertness)

The client's needs should be the central starting point in a financial service provider's service delivery process, not the question of what to do to achieve its own business goals.

For financial service providers, this means that their primary goal should be to fulfill their mission in the original sense of the word "financial service provider," namely, to serve their clients. Serving means asking oneself what helps one's clients and what is good for them, as well as what contribution can be made to improve the client's situation. What does the customer need? What serves the customer? These two key questions must be answered, and then the range of services must be aligned with the needs of the customer in order to become credible to the customer. The question of what serves the offering company should be answered downstream. The underlying expectation here is that a company that serves the customer well earns well. A major cause of financial service providers being perceived as untrustworthy is the customer perception that the financial sector is hermetic and lacks transparency (Fleishman 2014).

3.4 Fair Prices (Fairness)

The basic prerequisite for the long-term existence of a financial services company is economic success. This includes collecting appropriate prices for its services and products.

In terms of the definition of credibility, it would initially suffice to communicate prices transparently – regardless of whether they are reasonable. However, it can be assumed that few clients are willing to permanently pay prices that are too high. Accordingly, the financial service provider should charge its clients reasonable prices – prices that objectively correspond to the value of the service provided. The author is convinced that for every business there is an appropriate, optimal, fair price where the provider is paid well for his service and the service recipient pays a good and fair price for the service received. Whenever one of the two partners – be it the customer or the service provider – tries to shift this price level in his or her favor, an imbalance is created that may not be noticed in the short term but undermines credibility and trust on both sides in the long term and thus works against the economic success of the business.

3.5 Compliance with Legal Requirements and Framework Conditions (Trustworthiness)

Compliance with legal requirements is often not considered when assessing credibility. On the one hand, it is perceived as inconvenient because it requires a second effort, and on the other hand, it hinders success because it involves costs. At the same time, consistent compliance with legal requirements is of elementary importance for gaining credibility. These requirements serve not only the legal protection of the customer but also the legal protection of the company – an aspect that is often overlooked – and thus support the connection between company and customer. From the company's point of view, it should therefore be in the company's own interest to observe and comply with legal requirements with the aim of protecting the interests of the customer. Consistent compliance with the protection provisions increases credibility vis-à-vis third parties.

4 What About the Credibility of Financial Service Providers in Practice?

How do financial service providers manage to implement these characteristics to achieve credibility in practice? For each characteristic, the author describes a positive and a negative example from his consulting activities as follows:

4.1 Focus on Core Mission and Core Competence (Expertness)

4.1.1 Positive

One of the leading asset managers in the German-speaking region has its origins in asset management. The core competence of the founders lies in the analysis of securities and the construction of security portfolios. Over the years, the company has further focused its approach and developed a unique investment process that leads to excellent results for its clients.

The manager was confronted with a special catalogue of sustainability criteria to be taken into account in the context of a tender. The manager dealt with the catalogue of requirements in detail, explored the given scope for interpretation by means of targeted questions, and subsequently expressed that – if there would be further restrictions – he would no longer be able to offer his service, as otherwise he would have to deviate from his basic convictions ("core mission") and would not be able to implement his management approach ("core competence").

4.1.2 Negative

A bank from the cooperative sector that has its origins in the classic banking business, i.e., payment transactions, deposit, and lending business, and still performs well for its customers in these product fields today. Instead of focusing on its core competencies, the bank has expanded its range of services and also offers security business – advisory and asset management. The bank lacks the qualified staff required for a core competence as well as the excellent investment process required for a core competence, which is difficult to imitate. As a result, the bank almost exclusively uses the products of the umbrella organization in advising wealthy clients. Regrettably, these are in the last quintile in a sector comparison (Kremer 2020). The client – unknowingly – bears the damage.

4.2 Honest and Clear Communication of the Service Offer (Trustworthiness)

4.2.1 Positive

Another independent asset manager communicates his services in an exemplary, clear, and honest manner. In this specific case, this was demonstrated by the fact that the manager not only explains his offer in great detail in the "acquisition meeting," explaining the in-house investment process in an understandable way, but also addresses the fact that the results achieved in the past in the context of portfolio management are no guarantee for future results and thus also presents the limits of his own performance to the client. The financial service provider does not limit itself to positive aspects, but paints a comprehensive, honest picture of its own performance.

4.2.2 Negative

A bank from the cooperative sector tells its customers that although it offers products from the group of companies, it is fundamentally independent in the selection and offer of products. It thus suggests to its customers that it cannot only select the best products for its customers but also does so. Deposits that – as in the case of one of our clients – contain more than 80% average-quality products from our own group of companies speak the opposite language.

4.3 *Alignment of the Range of Services with the Needs of the Customer (Expertness)*

4.3.1 Positive

Once again, it is the abovementioned asset manager that stands out. The initial situation was the mandate in which the deposit of special sustainability guidelines was of great importance. These were formulated in such a way that there was a need for clarification regarding their implementation. While in almost all cases that have been presented with this case for analysis there were no or few questions, the mentioned administrator drilled down into the details of the topic and named to the client the scope for interpretation that needed to be clarified.

The honest effort to identify the client's needs as best as possible and thus also to be able to cover them within the framework of a solution was associated with a significant additional effort on the part of the financial service provider and, for the client, with the realization that there are enormous differences with regard to the willingness of financial service providers to align themselves with the client's needs.

4.3.2 Negative

In an identical initial situation, we experienced a private bank that assured the client in a personal conversation that it understood the sustainability guidelines and would also take them into account and implement them within the framework of its investment management. When asked how the process for implementation was organized within the institution, the bank failed to give a precise answer. There was no serious discussion of the client's needs.

4.4 *Fair Prices (Fairness)*

4.4.1 Positive

A bank belonging to an insurance group made us an excellent offer for our client in the course of a tendering process, combined with the indication that the bank did not want to renegotiate and therefore made the best possible offer from the outset.

The bank's chosen path of offering customers the best price has increased the credibility and thus the attractiveness of the bank by leaps and bounds. Especially since the offer was among the best in a comparison of numerous other condition offers and thus it was recognizable for the customer that the bank followed its words with deeds.

4.4.2 Negative

It is noticeable that almost all providers in the asset management sector do not offer fixed price models, but set the price on a case-by-case basis – depending on additional factors such as further business potential, reputation, negotiating skills of the client, etc. This is despite the fact that the providers generally do not offer individualized but standardized investment solutions.

While intensive discussions are held, for example, with the seller when buying a property and the price is negotiated intensively, this does not happen for the most part when investing in securities. This is surprising because the investment of one's own assets is a far-reaching entrepreneurial decision. Particularly in the case of entrepreneurial decisions, detailed consideration of the costs incurred in advance is of great importance. And entrepreneurial decisions that have already been made must be reviewed on an ongoing basis, and the costs incurred must also be considered and renegotiated if necessary.

Clients sometimes entrust banks and asset managers with sums in the tens of millions without being clear about how much they are actually paying for the service of the respective provider. The relative percentage is negotiated. The absolute amount is not taken into consideration. It is striking that banks interpret the legal requirements for cost transparency differently and as a result customers are shown different cost rates for identical condition offers from the providers.

During price negotiations with a major international bank, we experienced that the bank only provided the legally required cost transparency after several requests. Although the legislator stipulates that the costs must be stated in concrete amounts, the costs were initially only published in relation to the assets, i.e., as a percentage. An attempt to get banks to create cost transparency on the basis of a scheme provided by us was rejected by an international private bank, with the argument that it was not allowed to do so for regulatory reasons.

Financial service providers have been required under the European Markets in Financial Instruments Directive II to provide ex ante cost information for customers as of January 3, 2018 (European Parliament and of the Council 2014).

The Federal Financial Supervisory Authority rightly asks whether this is a "paper tiger or an important step towards an informed investor" (Boehm and Loff 2018) since clients often do not understand this document. Even the difference between service and product costs is not understandable for many. Another complicating factor is that the presentation of costs varies from bank to bank and provider to provider. No uniform standard seems to have been established so far, or there do not seem to be any precise specifications from the legislative side. It is rare to see providers detailing and explaining their costs on their own initiative – even when asked to do so.

4.5 Compliance with Legal Requirements and Framework Conditions (Trustworthiness)

4.5.1 Positive

A positive example is a private bank that complied with all regulatory and legal requirements during the advisory process, repeatedly pointing out that it had to comply with the legal requirements and that it would otherwise not be possible to establish a business relationship.

Even if this is occasionally perceived by customers as laborious and bureaucratic, the credibility of the provider perceived by the customer increases noticeably as a result. The customer deduces from this that the provider also behaves in a legally compliant manner in other areas and is thus a reliable partner.

4.5.2 Negative

A bank from the cooperative sector deprived a client of her legal protection. The client in need of protection was classified as a professional client, although it should have been recognizable that the expertise required for this was not available. The classification was made once and was not updated over the years. The consequences of this classification, in particular the significantly reduced level of protection, were not explained to the client. The actions of the financial service provider lead to a financial loss for the client that could have been reduced if the legal framework conditions had been adhered to.

5 New Approaches Are Needed!

The abovementioned examples from advisory practice show that a lack of credibility leads to considerable economic damage – especially on the part of the client – undermines the trust between financial market actor and client, and leads to a threat to the stability of the financial market. Strengthening the credibility of financial service providers should therefore be in everyone's overriding interest. To this end, it is necessary to develop standards that increase the credibility of financial service providers. The author gives five examples below of how credibility can be lived in practice.

5.1 *Focus on Core Mission and Core Competence (Expertness)*

Financial service providers make their core mission and core competence visible by publishing them and making them accessible to their stakeholders.

Our core mission is to . . .
Our core competence is . . .

They also have to make clear which services they do not offer. For example, an asset manager might see its core mission as preserving and growing its clients' assets and its core competence as having a unique investment process and implementing it stringently with qualified staff. Services that are not offered could be advised to clients with regard to succession issues or the valuation of real estate assets and/or the optimization of the profitability of real estate assets as well as foundation advice for foundations and much more.

5.2 *Honest and Clear Communication of the Service Offer (Trustworthiness)*

The financial service provider undertakes to present his services in a detailed, comprehensible, and honest manner within the framework of a "code of ethics." He hands out this code of ethics to his clients, thus making himself verifiable, and also offers his clients that they can contact an independent body if they have questions about his services and his offer and that they can also get references if they wish.

5.3 *Alignment of the Range of Services with the Needs of the Customer (Expertness)*

The financial service provider in turn undertakes within the framework of a "code of ethics" not to offer its clients any services that do not meet the client's needs. He also hands out this code of ethics to his clients and also offers his clients that they can have audited the service offered by an independent body.

5.4 *Fair Prices (Fairness)*

Introduction of a "fair price code": The financial service provider undertakes to charge customers' identical prices for comparable services. In addition, he undertakes to ensure that the price performance level offered is fair in a competitive comparison.

5.5 *Compliance with Legal Requirements and Framework Conditions (Trustworthiness)*

The special position of the financial industry and "the "intangibility" of the services provided have always led to the assumption that banks are not comparable with other business enterprises" (Gietl and Gittfried 2005, p. 7). The result is that "many service providers have not yet necessarily classified aspects such as process throughput times or reliability as quality criteria" (Gietl and Gittfried 2005, p. 7). A new way for banks and service providers could be to underpin the emphasis on reliability or compliance with the legal framework externally through certification. The author is not aware of any approaches to this so far. So this could also be a way to gain a competitive advantage.

Financial service providers could go new ways here – with the support of experienced consulting firms – and thus promote compliance with the legal framework.

6 Summary and Outlook

Credibility and the resulting trust between persons and institutions involved are the essential basis of a stable and functioning financial market. Lack of credibility causes considerable financial damage and endangers the stability of the financial system. It is therefore all the more remarkable that the attainment of credibility on the part of the players in the financial market is predominantly given little attention. In the literature, too, there is comparatively little discussion of credibility and, in particular, its operationalization.

New approaches and also new providers are needed here that "make the financial system servant again" and whose "economic activity has targeted good as its goal" (Bolsinger and Hanheiser 2020, p. 4).

In the question of the causes for a lack of integrity and resulting credibility in the financial sector, the role of the framework-creating political and state institutions is also largely neglected. Only if these are credible will providers in the financial market take credibility seriously. An example of this is the European Central Bank, which buys bonds from states and companies as part of its monetary policy without checking whether they comply with the "Charter of Fundamental Rights of the European Union." The central bank, which creates framework conditions for the financial market, thus violates the framework conditions created for it by the European Parliament and Commission (Bolsinger 2017).

6.1 Credibility Is also Elementary for State Institutions and Their Leaders

> The most essential quality for leadership is not perfection but credibility. People must be able to trust you (Rick Warren quoted after Maxwell 2011).

The damage caused by a lack of integrity in the financial sector is immense. The customer pays the bill in the form of higher prices and poor performance, which can lead to a loss of assets.

The provider is apparently smarter than the customer. Through this practice, he manages to assert his interests without the customer noticing that his, i.e., the customer's, interests play a subordinate role. This is supported and accompanied by a regulatory system that does not protect clients enough and does not itself comprehensively adhere to the given rules of the game.

The result is a system in which the powerful can abuse the weak. It is time for new financial service providers and consultants to emerge that are credible and whose real core concern is to serve their clients. It is not the regulatory framework alone that will achieve this but also the hearts of the people acting. Credible entrepreneurs and employees are the key to this.

> The question is not whether we have enough qualified people to do it. The question is whether they have enough credibility (Berthold Leibinger quoted after Müller 2012, p. 146).

References

Barney JB, Hesterly WS (2015) Strategic management and competitive advantage: concepts and cases. 5th ed., global ed. Boston Munich: Pearson

Boehm F, Loff A (2018) Cost transparency - Costs and charges disclosure: a paper tiger or an important step towards more clarity for investors? BaFin. Available at: https://www.bafin.de/SharedDocs/Veroeffentlichungen/EN/Fachartikel/2018/fa_bj_1807_Kostentransparenz_en.html. Accessed 28 April 2022

Bolsinger HJ (2017) Petition No 0429/2017 by Harald J. Bolsinger (German) on the compliance of the European Central Bank with the EU Charter of Fundamental Rights. Available at: https://www.europarl.europa.eu/petitions/en/petition/content/0429%252F2017/html/missinglink. Accessed 27 April 2022

Bolsinger HJ (2022) Herausforderungen im Nexus digitaler Entwicklung. In: Schweer MKW (ed) Facetten des Vertrauens und Misstrauens. Springer Fachmedien Wiesbaden, Wiesbaden, pp 355–366. https://doi.org/10.1007/978-3-658-29047-4_18

Bolsinger H, Hanheiser B (2020) FOUNDERS 4 FUTURE : Start up with deep impact! Available at: https://opus4.kobv.de/opus4-fhws/frontdoor/index/index/docId/1797. Accessed 27 April 2022

DiPiazza SA, Eccles RG (2002) Building public trust: the future of corporate reporting. New York: John Wiley & Sons Available at: http://www.123library.org/book_details/?id=5908. Accessed 26 April 2022

Eisend M (2003) Glaubwürdigkeit in der Marketingkommunikation: Konzeption, Einflussfaktoren und Wirkungspotenzial, 1st edn. Dt. Univ.-Verl (Gabler Edition Wissenschaft Marketing-Management), Wiesbaden

European Parliament and of the Council (2014) Directive 2014/65/EU of the European parliament and of the council of 15 May 2014 on markets in financial instruments and amending Directive 2002/92/EC and Directive 2011/61/EU. Available at: https://eur-lex.europa.eu/legal-content/EN/TXT/PDF/?uri=CELEX:02014L0065-20160701&rid=1. Accessed 28 April 2022

Fleishman H (2014) Finanzdienstleister im Reputation stief, Fleishman Hillard Germany. Available at: https://fleishmanhillard.de/2014/06/finanzdienstleister-kommen-nicht-aus-dem-reputationstief/. Accessed 26 April 2022

Gietl G, Gittfried N (2005) Qualitätsmanagement in Banken. Hanser (Pocket power), München Wien

Giffin K (1967) The contribution of studies of source credibility to a theory of interpersonal trust in the communication process. Psychol Bull 68(2):104–120

Glare PGW (ed) (2012) Oxford Latin dictionary, 2nd edn. Oxford University Press, Oxford

Hilligos B, Rieh SY (2008) Developing a unifying framework of credibility assessment: construct, heuristics, and interaction in context. Inf Process Manag 44:1467–1484

Hovland CI, Weiss W (1951) The influence of source credibility on communication effectiveness. Public Opin Q 15(4):635–650

Hovland CI, Janis IL, Kelley HH (1953) Communication and persuasion: psychological studies of opinion change. Yale University Press, Westport, Conn

Kremer D (2020) ‚DWS und andere im Vergleich: Der Anleger-Frust mit deutschen Fonds‘, FAZ. NET. Available at: https://www.faz.net/aktuell/finanzen/meine-finanzen/sparen-und-geld-anlegen/dws-co-der-anleger-frust-mit-deutschen-fonds-16906725.html. Accessed 30 March 2022

Lis B, Korchmar S (2013a) Digitales Empfehlungsmarketing. Springer Fachmedien Wiesbaden, Wiesbaden. https://doi.org/10.1007/978-3-658-01008-9

Lis B, Korchmar S (2013b) Digitales Empfehlungsmarketing: Konzeption, Theorien und Determinanten zur Glaubwürdigkeit des Electronic Word-of-Mouth (EWOM). Springer Fachmedien Wiesbaden Imprint: Springer Gabler (Digitales Empfehlungsmarketing), Wiesbaden

Lübbert F (2020) Edelman Trust Barometer 2020, Edelman Deutschland. Available at: https://www.edelman.de/research/edelman-trust-barometer-2020. Accessed 26 April 2022

Maxwell JC (2009) ‚Don‘t Bankrupt Your Leadership!‘, John Maxwell, 4 March. Available at: https://www.johnmaxwell.com/blog/dont-bankrupt-your-leadership/ Accessed 9 April 2022

Maxwell JC (2011) The five levels of leadership: proven steps to maximize your potential, 1st edn. Center Street, New York

Müller EB (2012) Charisma - mit Strategie und Persönlichkeit zum Erfolg: der Charisma Code, 1st edn. Haufe, Freiburg Munich

Nawratil U (1997) Glaubwürdigkeit in der sozialen Kommunikation. Available at: https://doi.org/10.1007/978-3-663-07905-7. Accessed 28 March 2022

Reinmuth M (2009) ‘Vertrauen und Wirtschaftssprache: Glaubwürdigkeit als Schlüssel für erfolgreiche Unternehmenskommunikation’, in Die Sprache der Wirtschaft. 2009th edn. VS Verlag für Sozialwissenschaften, pp. 127–145

Thommen J-P (2003) Glaubwürdigkeit und Corporate Governance, 2nd edn. Versus Verl, Zürich

Fundamental Rights in the Core Business of the ECB: Still No Issue

Harald J. Bolsinger

Würzburg 01/2023 Harald J. Bolsinger
Fundamental Rights in the Core Business of the ECB: Still No Issue!
Experience with the EU petition 429/2017—Part II

Abstract The European Union petition 0429/2017 wants to make the European Central Bank apply the EU Charter of Fundamental Rights in their whole core business consequently. The petition has been brought forward by Harald J. Bolsinger from Germany. In this second article, he describes backgrounds and developments around the petition until the beginning of 2023. The petition, submitted on May 8, 2017, addressed the investment policy of the ECB. Audits of violations of EU Fundamental Rights, it claimed, should be specifically included into the eligibility for EU-owned assets. As Bolsinger explains, the ECB is still involved in violations of the Charter of Fundamental Rights of the European Union through possession and trading of ethically very questionable assets.

1 The EU Petition 429/2017

1.1 Healing Eurosystem's Ethical Blindness

It is long overdue to oblige the global financial sector to comply with fundamental normative frameworks of humanity. These include, for example, the UN Charter of Human Rights but also the regional EU Charter of Fundamental Rights and the Paris Climate Agreement. Banks and investment companies have an indirect influence on

H. J. Bolsinger (✉)
Technical University of Applied Sciences Würzburg-Schweinfurt (THWS), Würzburg, Germany
e-mail: harald.bolsinger@thws.de

H. J. Bolsinger et al. (eds.), *The European Central Bank and Its Role in a Sustainable Finance System*, Sustainable Finance, https://doi.org/10.1007/978-3-031-24478-0_6

a large scale on the business conduct of the real economy through the financing of companies and investments in corresponding projects. Central banks have the greatest influence and, at the same time, the greatest responsibility, since they do not only serve as role models for commercial banks but also have a massive influence on their financing and investment behavior and, in addition, conduct transactions on the financial markets themselves. In the European Union, the ECB is an outstanding example of this responsibility of central banks. As an institution of the European Union, the ECB is fully committed to complying with the EU Charter of Fundamental Rights—at least in theory at present—because in practice this commitment and responsibility has still not been reflected in a principled monetary policy of the ECB since its foundation. The monetary policy instruments of this central bank do not operate fully within the guard rails of the EU Charter of Fundamental Rights, but rather ignore ethical controversies and fundamental rights risks inherent in assets in the ECB's portfolio to the greatest extent possible. To change this and not let the Eurosystem contradict the political will of the European Parliament and the Commission, EU petition 0429/2017 was submitted. In the 2021 paper "Fundamental Rights in the Core Business of the ECB: No Issue?!—Experience with the EU Petition 429/2017" in the volume *The European Central Bank as a Sustainability Role Model* (https://doi.org/10.1007/978-3-030-55450-7), the background, history, motivation for submitting the petition in 2017, and its status at the end of 2019 were explained. This article picks up there and continues the experiences in the further course of the political handling of the petition until the end of 2022. It continues the picture from the perspective of petitioner Harald J. Bolsinger and can be understood as testimony to the fact that all parties involved—the ECB, the European Parliament, and the European Commission—are now aware of the problem in its full extent, not at least due to the petition, and could very easily remedy it, which has not happened in the slightest way even after more than 4 years' time.

The original idea that it would be sufficient to point out this easily understandable and obvious grievance of the Eurosystem's ethical blindness to have it politically healed has changed in the meantime. Rather, it requires the genuine will in the hearts of top decision-makers to *really* implement European values enshrined in the Charter consistently in all policy areas for the benefit of all citizens. The actual handling of the seemingly politically inconvenient petition has become a yardstick for this attitude of the heart because the petition is neither one-sidedly politically colored, nor ideologically charged in one direction. It is quite simply about implementing the fundamental rights that have already been established—without wanting to renegotiate them. Basically, it is about the question of whether all European institutions should work equally to protect and promote the fundamental rights or whether there should be one institution that can rise above them without restriction with pretextual arguments about price stability—to the detriment of the entire European Union and to its own detriment in terms of credibility. See for yourself what has happened in the context of the petition since the last article. Cited statements in original German language are all translated by the author to English for this article.

1.2 *The Petition in a Nutshell*

The original petition was submitted on May 8, 2017, in German language and can be found in Annex A.1 of the 2021 predecessor article or online under www.wirtschaftsethik.biz/zentralbank. The petition was registered under the number 0429/2017 entitled "Compliance of the European Central Bank with the EU Charter of Fundamental Rights" on May 15, 2017. It shows up the simple problem, which has not changed at all since 2017 and which exists since the very first day the ECB started to work: ECB's core business does decisively not examine EU Fundamental Rights violations at all! As an example, for the large-scale influence on the EU citizens—and even the people of the whole world—that must be changed, the petition shows the problem on the base of collaterals. All banks of the Eurozone must obtain credit from the ECB. The ECB provides such credit against collaterals. The volume of the "eligible marketable assets" for use as collateral is 16,894.8 billion € end of Q3 2022 (see https://www.ecb.europa.eu/paym/coll/charts/html/index.en.html). It includes government securities, bank and corporate bonds, asset-backed securities, and other marketable assets. This means it has an incredibly large influence on the EU single market and the EU citizens. The ECB's eligibility criteria for collateral and other assets do still not include any audits for violations of the European Charter of Fundamental Rights, so there is a total ethical blindness in the EU financial market regarding inherent EU values! For the ECB and all European banks! The petition proved by ESG controversy scans that about 20% of the ECB's "eligible marketable assets" are involved in severe or very severe ethical controversies (see www.wirtschaftsethik.biz/centralbank)! Based on that, the petition asks for simple transparency for potential violations of the European Charter of Fundamental Rights and actions to stop this monetary policy misalignment, as it really should be possible to achieve price stability without accepting violations of fundamental rights by banks, corporates, and governments. The solution is simple: Alignment with EU Fundamental Rights must be specifically included into the eligibility criteria for all ECB-owned assets—also the assets that the ECB buys in their purchase programs.

2 Moving on with the Newly Staffed EU Committees

As one can see in the 2021 predecessor article, the political handling of the petition was as exciting as a thriller, and the impression comes up that the political responsible of the electoral term 2014–2019 did not want to act at all in that topic. The Committee on Petitions of the new parliamentary term, on the other hand, had put the issue on the agenda as soon as its business began. So, there was justified hope that the new EU Committee on Petitions chaired by Dolors Montserrat will bring change together with new President of the European Commission Ursula von der Leyen and new ECB President Christine Lagarde, as all of them positioned themselves as advocates of fundamental rights at the beginning of their duty. Let's put an eye on it and how the viewpoints of the new decision-makers have changed in accordance with the petition.

2.1 Experiences with the Committee on Petitions

On November 11, 2019, the petition was discussed again in the newly constituted Petitions Committee after an explanation and comments by the petitioner together with Jens Minnemann as one of the actually 78 supporters of the petition. In advance, the Petitions Committee has got the following speech script, which made the main points as clear as possible in the shortest possible form:

The Problem: Still nearly unchanged

ECBs core business does not take EU fundamental rights into account

- The ECB still seeingly becomes owner of securities that undermine the EU Charter of Fundamental Rights with severe ethical controversies.
- volume of the "eligible marketable assets" for use as collateral is at the moment 13,980.9 Billion € (Source: ECB, Data of 10/2019). → Very large influence on the EU single market and EU citizens.
- ECB's **eligibility criteria** for collateral and other assets **do not include compliance with the European Charter of Fundamental Rights.** → Ethical blindness of financial market for EU values.
- ESG-controversy scans prove, that 20 % (Data source for 2017/2018: oekom for 2019: vigeo eiris & imug bond sonar) of the ECB's "eligible marketable assets" are **involved in severe ethical controversies!** → ECB is part of **financing** companies that are defecting fundamental rights. → This stabilizes and **enhances unethical business practices in the EU**.

The Solution

Include compliance with EU Fundamental Rights into eligibility criteria for assets that the ECB can own

- It is already the duty of the ECB as an EU institution to respect fundamental rights all-encompassing in its business conduct.
- Art. 6 (1) TEU: unconditional legal binding nature of the Charter.
- Art. 51/52 Charter: unconditional legal binding for the ECB.
- **The TFEU does not grant independence of the EU Charter of Fundamental rights!** Respecting fundamental rights is just an existing regulatory MUST for all EU institutions. Fundamental rights are the limits of all actions, also for the ECB's actions.
- **Respecting fundamental rights does not violate the institutional independence of the ECB**, is no political instruction and is not a matter of exclusive competence on monetary policy!
- You are the Guardians of the Charter of Fundamental Rights: **Please** help the ECB to comply with these codified European values.

Comments to the reply of the European Commission

- 'The Commission cannot take further action as the petition is related to policy areas where the ECB has exclusive competence and is granted independence by the TFEU.'
  → No EU institution is independent of Fundamental Rights! **The Commission can define eligibility criteria guidelines** for compliance with EU Fundamental Rights.
- 'The petition should be addressed to the ECB.'
  → **Petitions are a matter for the petition committee.** In their answer, the ECB urges political authorities (= the petition committee) to 'define, agree and promote' ethical minimum standards to implement in their everyday work.
- 'Moreover, it has to be kept in mind that the ECB is accountable for its policies, including through regular reporting and dialogue with the European Parliament (Article 284 TFEU).' → **It should become a standard that the ECB reports on fundamental rights compliance** to the Parliament regularly.

Comments to the reply of the ECB

- The ECB is aware of the effects of their assets purchase and collateral eligibility: they talk about positive effects by buying good (ecological) assets and therefore know about the negative effects as well. **The ECB even asks for regulation in these aspects in their answer!**

Summary

- The Lisbon Treaties make the EU Charter of Fundamental Rights a directly applicable primary law in all European institutions. All the ECB's operations as a European institution must therefore comply with the codified values of the Charter of Fundamental Rights. The ECB's responses to the petition shows that it is waiting for political action.
- **Please**—the European Parliament, as guardian of fundamental rights, must act based on this petition and persuade the Commission & ECB to finally remedy the biggest systemic error in the European financial market system."

After an exciting debate of which a video documentation is available online (see https://www.europarl.europa.eu/streaming/?event=20191111-1500-COMMITTEE-PETI&start=2019-11-11T14:08:49Z&end=2019-11-11T16:29:36Z&language=en), the Petitions Committee resolved the previous mixing with a completely inappropriate other petition, closed this other petition, and kept the fundamental rights petition 429/2017 open—combined with the intention to submit the demands for fundamental rights compliance of the ECB to the other newly constituted European Parliament Committees and the ECB under new leadership for further political treatment and opinion. A renewed inquiry to the ECB was confirmed in a letter from the chair of the Committee on Petitions dated January 14, 2020. Over 3 months later on April 28, 2020, the Petitions Committee and the two German MEPs (Ms. Müller, and Mr. Jahr, CDU) were asked what the situation was. After a direct follow-up by the MEP office of Peter Jahr on May 20, 2020, the

Secretariat of the Petitions Committee sent a reprint of the letter to Ms. Lagarde on May 27, 2020, to the petitioner:

"Subject: Petition No. 0429/2017 by Harald J. Bolsinger (German) on the compliance of the European Central Bank with the EU Charter of Fundamental Rights

Dear President,

I would like to inform you that members took note of the letter by the European Central Bank, DG International and European Relations, of 22 June 2018 on the above-mentioned petition. Please find attached a reaction on the letter from the petitioner-dated 27 June 2018.

Further, I would like to inform you that, in the meeting of 11 November 2019, the Committee on Petitions has again examined petition 0429/2017. Please find attached the petitioner's presentation that he gave in the meeting. The members of the committee decided that the petition would remain open and asked for an updated opinion from you on the matter raised by the petitioner, in particular on the question of compliance of the European Central Bank with the European Charter of Fundamental Rights.

We would appreciate any further information and comments you could offer on the matter. Should you require further information, please contact the Secretariat of the Committee on Petitions at [...]

Yours sincerely"

The letter was sent directly to the president of the European Central Bank, Ms. Christine Lagarde, on January 14 and included the speech script presented on November 11, 2019, in the Committee on Petitions. In May, according to the Petitions Committee, Christine Lagarde received an email reminder requesting a response. The new Committee on Economic and Monetary Affairs did not revisit the issue. This was raised at the committee meeting on November 11, 2019, but not recorded in the minutes as a decision. A request to the Petitions Committee Secretariat to still do this at their discretion was sent by the petitioner on May 27. Even at the beginning of August 2020, there was still no response from the ECB. Peter Jahr's office inquired again about the status. On August 27, 2020, the Secretariat of the Committee on Petitions forwarded the ECB's reply, dated August 5, 2020, which was not signed by the direct addressee Christine Lagarde, but by the ECB director general of International and European Relations:

"Re: Petition No 0429/2017 by Harald J. Bolsinger (German) on the compliance of the European Central Bank with the EU Charter of Fundamental Rights

Honourable Member of the European Parliament, dear Ms. Montserrat,

Thank you for your letter seeking further information from the European Central Bank (ECB) regarding its reply to Petition No 0429/2017 by Harald J. Bolsinger (German) on the compliance of the ECB with the Charter of Fundamental Rights of the European Union (hereafter "Charter").

The ECB's primary objective, as mandated by the Treaty on the Functioning of the European Union (the Treaty), is to ensure price stability over the medium term. In order to achieve this primary objective, the ECB and the national central banks of the Eurosystem have at their disposal a number of tools as indicated in the Statute of the ECB and ESCB (hereafter the "Statute"). Credit operations with credit institutions and other market participants are one of these core tools, as stated in Article 18 of the Statute. The eligibility of assets as collateral for such credit operations is thus primarily guided by considerations regarding the monetary policy objective and appropriate risk management—to shield the Eurosystem against potential losses. The Eurosystem ensures that collateral assets serve the monetary policy objective and that the Eurosystem is adequately protected against risks, and reserves the right to limit or reject the mobilisation of certain assets. Under Article 19 of the Statute, and within the limits set by the Council as referred to in this Article, the Eurosystem may require credit institutions to hold minimum reserves in pursuance of monetary policy objectives. Minimum reserves are not collateralised since they constitute a deposit made by credit institutions which are subject to the Eurosystem's minimum reserve requirements with their respective Eurosystem national central banks. No counterparty is obliged to hold collateral as a result of it being subject to minimum reserves.

That being said, and as already mentioned in a recent reply to a written question from MEP Daly (See letter from the ECB President to Ms Clare Daly, MEP, on the Charter of Fundamental Rights, available at https://www.ecb.europa.eu/pub/pdf/other/ecb.mepletter200619_Daly~cee67c7de1.en.pdf*), the ECB is an addressee of the Charter of Fundamental Rights within the limits of Article 51 thereof. The ECB respects the rights, observes the principles and promotes the application of the Charter, in accordance with its powers and respecting the limits of the powers of the Union as conferred on it in the Treaties (Treaty on European Union and Treaty on the Functioning of the European Union). At the same time, the precise and limited mandate and powers conferred on the ECB by the Treaties, as well as the limits to the powers of the Union conferred on it by the Treaties, imply that while the ECB is an addressee of the Charter, it does not automatically have an obligation to enforce the Charter vis-à-vis the issuers of securities it considers eligible for use in its monetary policy operations. While recognising that the matter may be complex, the following considerations help to substantiate this view.*

- *First, private corporations such as the issuers named by the Petitioner in his initial petition do not fall directly within the scope of the Charter, which specifies that it is addressed to the institutions, bodies, offices and agencies of the Union with due regard for the principle of subsidiarity and to the Member States only when they are implementing Union law. These corporations, however, are instead subject to certain rules applicable to their conduct within the relevant jurisdictions, which may include rules set out in directly applicable EU regulations or other legal acts. The ECB cannot subject the eligibility of collateral to conditions which would effectively extend the scope of the Charter beyond the limits set in Article 51 thereof, and its own powers beyond the mandate established in the Treaties.*
- *Second, the authoritative assessment of alleged breaches of fundamental rights under the Charter, or other rules in EU legal acts that may be linked to the*

protection of these fundamental rights, falls within the remit of the relevant regulatory authorities and, ultimately, the competent national and EU courts, not within those of the ECB or of private self-authenticated institutions. The ECB cannot substitute itself for competent EU or national courts and authorities by assessing and, as the case may be, indirectly sanctioning EU corporations—to which the Charter does not even apply directly—for alleged breaches. The ECB also cannot simply defer to the findings of private self-authenticated sources such as those proposed by the Petitioner.

Therefore, the ECB cannot defer the eligibility of assets in its monetary policy operations to the opinion of a private entity regarding issuers' compliance with the Charter, as proposed by the Petitioner.

Yours sincerely"

The content of ECB's answer contradicts in some points the public pronouncements of Ms. President Lagarde on the subject, as she was discussing these days considering climate change risk issues in monetary policy. Therefore, in September 2020, the ECB's response letter was analyzed in an academic meeting with a panel of experts from the Weltethos (Global Ethic) Research Group on Finance and Economics, and a recommendation was drawn up for further political consideration as follows:

"Open letter on the European Central Bank (EU-Petition 0429/2017)

Dear Ms. Montserrat, Honorable members of the European Committee on Petitions,

as members of the Weltethos Research Group on Finance and Economics we are addressing this letter to you, and at the same time to the broader group of responsible people in European institutions, because an urgent course of action regarding the business conduct of the European Central Bank (ECB) must be openly discussed: The ECB is counteracting, with substantial parts of its core business, a sustainable strategy for the future of Europe.

In response to the petition of our research group member Prof. Dr. Harald J. Bolsinger to the EU Petitions Committee of the European Parliament ("Commitment of the European Central Bank to the EU Charter of Fundamental Rights" of 08.05.2017, Petition 0429/2017), the ECB returned a response letter which was sent on 05.08.2020. This letter clarifies why this issue at the ECB has still not been sufficiently addressed. In September 2020, we analyzed the written reply during a scientific convention with a body of experts from the Weltethos Research Group on Finance and Economics and we would like to share our assessment with you:

In the response, it is explicitly acknowledged that the ECB is obliged to respect the EU Charter of Fundamental Rights. It is further claimed that the ECB respects fundamental rights, checks that the principles are respected, and promotes their application: "The ECB respects the rights, observes the principles and promotes the application of the Charter".

This statement is simply wrong, as the ECB itself confirms that it does not carry out any fundamental rights compliance assessments of marketable assets or other securities, arguing that the Charter of Fundamental Rights is not applicable to transactions with private companies. "While the ECB is an addressee of the Charter, it does not automatically have an obligation to enforce the Charter vis-a-vis the issuers of securities it considers eligible for use in its monetary policy operations." The central bank is deliberately turning a blind eye to the evidence presented in the petition. With such a justification, any European institution would be allowed to buy and resell on a large scale, for example, environmentally destructive products made by slaves and produced by corrupt tax evaders, as long as there are no direct violations of the Charter of Fundamental Rights within the institution itself.

It is astonishing that the ECB does not check or presuppose any compliance with fundamental rights for marketable assets, although this would be legally possible in a simple way: "The eligibility of assets as collateral [. . .] is thus primarily guided by considerations regarding the monetary policy objective and appropriate risk management". "The Eurosystem [. . .] reserves the right to limit or reject the mobilisation of certain assets".

***The ECB is therefore knowingly failing to complete its basic due diligence and has confirmed so. Furthermore, it claims that it is not subject to this basic due diligence at all. From our point of view, this is a scandal and unworthy of the European Union.** Since the ECB itself does not carry out the check for fundamental rights compliance, the answer claims, as a precaution, that it also could not refer to external sustainability ratings from established rating agencies. „ECB cannot defer the eligibility of assets [. . .] to the opinion of a private entity regarding issuers' compliance with the Charter". This contradicts the fact that the ECB obtains ratings and services from Standard & Poor's, Moody's, BlackRock,* etc. *itself, or takes them into account in its risk assessments—especially when assessing marketable assets or even commercial banks. Furthermore, this statement suggests that the sustainability ratings of globally recognized rating agencies would not be reliable from the ECB's point of view, which is completely at odds with EU practice in relation to the new EU taxonomy for sustainable activities, as presented by the European Commission.*

*From our perspective, the response by the ECB's Director General of International & European Relations contradicts the public statements made by President Lagarde that sustainability issues—especially in connection with climate change—will be taken into account in monetary policy practice in the future. This is the most important point, since successful central bank action in the long term is based on consistent, uniform communication to ensure credibility. **Since the reply to the EU Committee on Petitions was not signed directly by the President**, but only by the Director General International & European Relations, **we recommend to directly address Mrs. Lagarde, with a request for a personal reply and statement, especially because she was directly and personally addressed in the Committee on Petitions' inquiry.***

In addition, the answer we received also contradicts public statements of other ECB leaders, such as those of Isabel Schnabel (Member of the Executive Board of the ECB). In her speech at the European Sustainable Finance Summit end of September 2020, Ms. Schnabel adopted the solution proposed by our research group member from the 2017 petition as a way for the ECB to counter climate *change and literally said: "**we could consider linking the eligibility of securities as collateral in our refinancing operations to the disclosure regime of the issuing firms.** Then the Eurosystem would only accept collateral if it is able to fully assess climate-related risks".*

These inconsistencies between the public announcements of ECB leaders and the response of the Director General of International & European Relations on such an important issue suggest a conflict within the ECB regarding potential changes in policy towards climate risk mitigation and, by extension, fundamental rights compliance risks. We therefore consider it essential to have an immediate and broad public political discussion on this issue, especially now.

***We recommend that the European Parliament's Committee on Petitions works to ensure that the ECB is required, for the first time in its history, to provide Parliament with transparency on fundamental rights compliance regarding all traded securities and assets—in particular for the $15 trillion of securities recognized as marketable collateral**—and then, in a second step, to respond to the call made by the ECB under the leadership of President Mario Draghi in its June 22nd, 2018 reply to the Committee on Petitions, where it itself states, „it is up to political authorities to define, agree and promote appropriate measures to address such issues. In this sense, the ECB welcomes the European Commission's action plan on financing sustainable growth".*

As the ECB's answers have so far impressively demonstrated, the ECB can only be persuaded to finally implement the Charter of Fundamental Rights in its operations, as all other European institutions have long since done, with the help of targeted commitments by the European Parliament and the European Commission. This does not contradict the mandate of the ECB, on the contrary, it is the only way to fulfill it properly.

With kind regards"

This recommendation was forwarded by the Global Ethic Institute's research group on Finance and Economics to the chair of the Petitions Committee as well as to other members of the EU Parliament including all political group chairs of the European Parliament in October 2020. There was no response to the recommendation from the Committee of Petitions. Nearly a whole year after that—in September 2021—the Petitions Committee chair and MEP Peter Jahr were asked for an update. Mr. Jahr had received confirmation from the Petitions Committee Secretariat that the petition was indeed last processed in 2020. He wanted to try putting the petition back on the agenda of the Committee so that it will finally be processed further.

2.2 Experiences with the Committee on Economic and Monetary Affairs

The relevant political groups also ignored the issue by not responding at all to the open letter. Only individual feedback from MEP Markus Ferber (CSU) was very informative, as he has been a member of the Committee on Economic and Monetary Affairs (ECON) since 2009, was elected first vice-chairman of the committee in 2014, and has been spokesman for the EPP Group in ECON since 2018. In his reply letter on November 3, 2020, he made clear: "The ECB is first and foremost committed to the objective of price stability and to the principle of market neutrality in its monetary policy actions. All other policy objectives to which the European Central Bank is dedicated must not stand in the way of these principles." In an honorary capacity, Mr. Ferber is also chairman of the Hanns Seidel Foundation, deeply linked to Christian Democracy in Bavaria. Hoping for a rethink that makes him act in the ECON, he received this replica directly from the petitioner combined with an appeal to take action:

"Petition 0429/2017—Your letter of 3.11.2020.

Dear Mr. Ferber,

Thank you very much for your response to our note on the initiative regarding the ECB. We are very pleased that you are fundamentally concerned with this weighty issue as our representative in Brussels. Of course, we have also brought the issue into the public consultation, in addition to the petition that has been available since 2017.

As an ordoliberal thinker with a Christian background, I am very saddened by the inaction of you in the role of the CSU member. It is not a question of the ECB taking "greater" account of the Charter of Fundamental Rights, but of taking it into account at all. You are trying the principle of "market neutrality" and refer to the European Treaties to boot, not even "questioning" the existing drawbacks. There is no such thing as market neutrality, since every market transaction necessarily has an impact. The existing treaties oblige the ECB in particular to act within the normative framework of the Charter of Fundamental Rights.

If we apply the facts to Bavaria, we could accept that BayernLB would be allowed to disregard the principles of the Bavarian constitution and do business with human traffickers and arms dealers, corrupt tax avoiders and ecological destroyers without any problems and without prior compliance checks. BayernLB, however, is far ahead of the ECB in practice because it is aware "that every investment and financing decision also has a social and environmental dimension." At the same time, it has defined detailed specifications for "critical and controversial business areas [...] which companies and projects [...] are excluded with regard to their negative social and environmental impact". We in Bavaria can show by this example alone in the EU how to do it right. But to do so, we must also be convinced that it is right to apply the existing rules of the game in all institutions without exception.

If you won't stand up for the simple demand to the ECB to live up to its duty of care and scrutiny with regard to the Charter of Fundamental Rights of the European Union, who will? You are a weighty representative in the EU Parliament for the ECON Committee and can put the issue on the agenda. Mr. Gualtieri has shown for your committee at the time that he has not even read or even understood the petition....

Yours sincerely

Harald J. Bolsinger"

The reply shows that there are banks out there—here in Bavaria in Germany as an example—that already do voluntarily what the ECB should do as a role model. The BayernLB is no specialized sustainability bank but tries to do things right by opening their eyes to ethical questions proactively. The communication with politicians in charge about these examples should lead to proactive thematization in the relevant committee of the European Parliament. In this case, there was only upon request a reply almost a year later in September 2021, in which Mr. Ferber reiterated that the ECB would be independent in monetary policy decisions within the scope of its mandate because the European treaties would be clear in the tasks of the European Central Bank. Mr. Ferber even stated that there is "a mandate to politicians to protect this very independence" of the ECB. Working with these answers is difficult, because in the petitions points the European treaties are just shown as not respected and politically responsible persons seem not to mind this with reference to a misinterpreted independence of the ECB. This shows a basic problem of the petition, as there can only be change, when political decision-makers start to perceive the problem and rethink seemingly simple truths about the independence of the ECB.

In March 2021, Gabriele Bischoff (SPD) responded to a direct citizen inquiry on the petition, which shows that there are indeed also decision-makers in the ECON perceiving the problem of the petition and working actively on a possible solution. Ms. Bischoff is a deputy member of the Committee on Economic and Monetary Affairs (ECON) and thus currently has a somewhat weightier role. She made it clear that the ECB "should not indirectly participate in the financing of human rights abuses" but also that "as an institution, it is independent from both EU institutions and member state governments." It was through Ms. Bischoff's response that we got to know about a parliamentary question to the president of the ECB in March 2020 to clarify whether the ECB follows the European Charter of Fundamental Rights when buying assets. Unfortunately, the Petitions Committee did not provide the petitioner with any information on this matter, although this inquiry could be traced back to the petition. Ms. Bischoff cited Ms. Lagarde's answer of June 2020 (available online here: https://www.ecb.europa.eu/pub/pdf/other/ecb.mepletter200619_Daly~cee67c7de1.en.pdf):

"Like all EU institutions, the ECB is an addressee of the Charter of Fundamental Rights. The ECB respects the rights, observes the principles and promotes the application thereof, in accordance with its powers and respecting the limits of the powers of the Union as conferred on it in the Treaties. This covers all the ECB's tasks in the fields of monetary policy and banking supervision, in its advisory capacity, as well as its role under the Treaty establishing the European Stability Mechanism (ESM) and Regulation (EU) No 472/2013.1. Reviewing the compatibility of the ECB's actions with the Charter is part of our internal legal scrutiny procedures, which are followed for all actions through which the ECB discharges its tasks. In addition, the conformity of the ECB's actions with the Charter is reviewable by the Court of Justice of the European Union, which has affirmed that the ECB acts in line with the Charter. In this context, I would like to point out that the ECB has a specific mandate and is assigned specific tasks under the Treaties, unlike the

Commission, which, as the guardian of the Treaties, is tasked with monitoring the application of EU law in general. The ECB's accountability to the European Parliament provides an additional channel to ensure such compliance."

Ms. Bischoff's answer to the citizen included as last point that the Court of Justice of the European Union had affirmed that the ECB would act in line with the Charter of Fundamental Rights, proven by the judgments in the cases "Frank Steinhoff and Others v European Central Bank, Case T-107/17" and "Alessandro Accorinti and Others v European Central Bank, Case T-79/13".

This answer to a citizen request suggests that Ms. Bischoff—and with her other members of the ECON—truly believes that the ECB's security trading charter compliance would be approved by the Court of Justice of the European Union (ECJ). Ms. Lagarde's sentence in her answer to the ECON "the Court of Justice of the European Union, [...] has affirmed that the ECB acts in line with the Charter" really can make the Committee on Economic and Monetary Affairs (ECON) believe that everything would be alright, and this would have been even proven by the highest EU court. Ms. Lagarde certainly did not intend to mislead ECON with her answer, yet the sentence may lead to it being misinterpreted, as it is worded very unhappily and ambiguously especially in the context of the petition's issues. When working through the court judgments that Ms. Lagarde has cited in the footnote of her letter to prove her statement, it turns out to be misleading in the context of the petition's claims. The claim in the context of "Frank Steinhoff and Others v European Central Bank, Case T-107/17" and Vereinigte Raiffeisenbanken Gräfenberg-Forchheim-Eschenau-Heroldsberg eG relates, on the one hand, to a different set of facts (here specifically the problem is about property rights) and, on the other hand, the Court of Justice of the European Union in its reasoning (see https://eur-lex.europa.eu/legal-content/EN/TXT/?uri=CELEX:62017TJ0107) makes quite clear, in the spirit of the petition, that the ECB *has to* comply with the Charter of Fundamental Rights completely: "Similarly, the special status conferred on the ECB within the institutional framework of the Treaties does not exempt it from the requirement to respect the fundamental rights of the Union or from its duty to contribute to the attainment of the objectives of the Union as set out in Articles 2, 3 and 6 TEU." The ECJ extends their statement with a remark that the right to property guaranteed by Article 17(1) of the Charter may be subject to restrictions justified by objectives of general interest, which draws attention to the fact that a balancing of interests can be acceptable in special cases. Certainly, it is not an objective of general interest of the European Union and of the ECB to promote companies that accept slave labor and child labor, engage in corruption and tax avoidance, or systematically destroy the environment. Regarding the petition, the ECB president's response to ECON is blurred and can result in a misleading nonchalance of the political responsible. Also in the claim "Alessandro Accorinti and Others v European Central Bank, Case T-79/13" (see https://eur-lex.europa.eu/legal-content/EN/TXT/?uri=CELEX:62013TJ0079) named by Ms. Lagarde, there is no reference to the criticism from the petition recognizable. It is simply not about the question that the Parliament had asked, namely, the fundamental rights compliance of the securities and assets traded and purchased by the ECB. But it is rather the case that here, too, the ECJ makes clear statements on the binding of the ECB by the Charter with regard to certain articles—here on the principle of equal treatment: "the principle of equal treatment, as enshrined in Articles 20 and 21 of the Charter of Fundamental Rights [. . .], which the ECB, as an EU institution, is required to observe as a superior rule of EU law protecting individuals."

Due to these reasons, the petitioner called attention on September 29, 2021, in a message to Ms. Bischoff directly that Ms. Lagarde's answer to the ECON could be misleading in the context of the petition's claims and that there is no holistic compliance with the Charter of Fundamental Rights certified by the ECJ at all. Also, the citizen that was in correspondence with Ms. Bischoff has sent out the following three clear questions to ECON members in March 2022 to make sure that they really reflect on the points of the petition:

- "Why are unethical issuers accepted by the ECB in the marketable assets and no fundamental rights conformity of the assets is checked at all, although according to Ms. Lagarde the EU Charter of Fundamental Rights "applies to all tasks of the ECB in the areas of monetary policy"?
- When will you, as the responsible committee in the European Parliament, demand detailed information from the ECB for the first time on the conformity with fundamental rights of all assets & securities held by the ECB?
- As can be seen from the course of the petition at https://www.wirtschaftsethik.biz/centralbank, so far you seem to have received only general insubstantial answers from Ms. Lagarde. You have never yet demanded an assessment of all securities held by the ECB, such as the petitioner has already sought at his own expense in 2017 for all marketable assets. Are you not the guardians of fundamental rights with a duty to demand real transparency?

I would appreciate answers to my three questions. Thank you very much for your efforts."

By this time at the latest, all ECON members can be said to be informed about the problem.

2.3 *Experiences with the European Commission*

Great hope for the petition's cause was placed in the appointment of Mairead McGuinness as Commissioner for Financial Stability, Financial Services, and Capital Markets. In January 2021, she was encouraged with this letter signed by Harald J. Bolsinger, Johannes Hoffmann, Ndidi Nnoli-Edozien, Bernd Villhauer, and Benedikt Hoffmann for the whole Weltethos Research Group Members on Finance and Economics, to create transparency about the ECB's fundamental rights compliance:

"[. . .] dear Ms. McGuinness,

aligning the financial system with sustainability is still in its infancy. We are convinced that you play a key role in the necessary change, as we intensively read about your actions for the green deal.

As members of the Weltethos Research Group on Finance and Economics we are addressing this letter to you, because an urgent course of action regarding the business conduct of the European Central Bank (ECB) must be openly discussed: The ECB is counteracting a sustainable strategy for the future of Europe with substantial parts of its core business. In response to the petition 0429/2017 ("Commitment of the European Central Bank to the EU Charter of Fundamental Rights") of our research group member Prof. Dr. Harald J. Bolsinger to the EU Petitions Committee, the ECB returned a response letter which shows, that itself confirms that it does not carry out any fundamental rights compliance assessments of marketable assets or other securities.

We recommend that the European Commission and the Parliament's Committee on Petitions work together to ensure that the ECB is required, for the first time in its history, to provide transparency on fundamental rights compliance regarding all traded securities and assets—in particular for the $15 trillion of securities recognized as marketable collateral—and then, in a second step, to respond to the call made by the ECB under the leadership of President Mario Draghi in its June 22nd, 2018 reply to the Committee on Petitions, where itself states, „it is up to political authorities to define, agree and promote appropriate measures to address such issues. In this sense, the ECB welcomes the European Commission's action plan on financing sustainable growth".

Sustainability worthy of its name includes the abandonment of externalization of costs to environmental, social and cultural commons. We need to make sure, that at least our financial markets stop financing destructive and with the EU Charter of Fundamental Rights non-compliant business actions.

We would love to hear you raising your voice to address this problem in general and the petition in particular. What is your position to petition 0429/2017? Would it be possible to invite you as a speaker to a scientific conference in Frankfurt in October this year?"

As it can be seen from the last sentence, Mairead McGuinness was asked to participate in the scientific conference planned for October 2021 that should take place in Frankfurt together with leading members of the Club of Rome. This conference is the basis for the present volume on the topic and should give her a chance to address the petition claims in a suitable context. End of August 2021—7 months later—we received a cancellation, which did not include any political position to the petition. In a reply, the conference committee asked for any representation or a simple video message as a contribution to the conference—but not even that had been made possible. Additionally, regarding transparency about the ECB's fundamental rights compliance, we have not become aware of any activities of the European Commission and its relevant commissioner until today. It was surprising and deeply disappointing that the new Commission continued the poor performance for the petition claims of their predecessors, because Ursula von der Leyen had praised in her application phase in her political guidelines for the next

European Commission 2019–2024 a “European Green Deal” and “An economy that works for people” (see https://ec.europa.eu/info/sites/default/files/political-guide lines-next-commission_en_0.pdf). As new president of the European Commission, she staged her inauguration exactly on the tenth anniversary of the Treaty of Lisbon and had held up the Charter of Fundamental Rights of the EU to the cameras of the news channels together with President of the European Council Charles Michel, the in January 2022 deceased President of the EU Parliament David Sassoli, and new ECB President Christine Lagarde (see https://www.tagesschau.de/multimedia/video/video-628293.html as an example of the German Tagesschau on December 1, 2019). Doing nothing about a fundamental complaint like the petition 429/2017 and even repeating the answer of the predecessor Commission in the style of “we are not responsible and cannot do anything” are embarrassing statements about the real importance of fundamental rights in the Eurosystem to the top decision-makers in the acting European Commission.

3 Additional Activities for and by the ECB

On October 10, 2019, the German Sustainability Council adopted in its recommendation to the Federal Government in point 10 the demand for a regulation of the ECB in the sense of the petition. The idea originates from the results of the Second Sustainable Finance Summit Germany in Frankfurt in 2018. The Sustainability Council went beyond the existing fundamental rights obligation and even demanded that the ECB must be bound by the principle of sustainability (see https://www.nachhaltigkeitsrat.de/wp-content/uploads/2019/10/2019-10-15_Stellungnahme_Sus tainable_Finance_Strategie_der_Bundesregierung.pdf). The point was discussed in a roundtable on that summit. Normally, you should be able to retrace the origin of such thoughts by publicly available documentation as background information about that roundtable. Its contribution was available on the website of the German Hub for Sustainable Finance some time. Unfortunately, all website contents of all contributors to the Hub for Sustainable Finance so far have been deleted in the meantime. With the establishment of the Sustainable Finance Advisory Board, the German Council for Sustainable Development had decided to close that initiative. The offer to take over the content of the hub website and thus also the documentation of this topic as a permanent dialog offering on the website of the Sustainable Finance Advisory Board was rejected. The value of third-party contributions to this core topic appears to be very low against this background. A request from September 2020 on behalf of the Research Group Finance and Economics of the Global Ethic Institute to make the emergence of the topic visible to the management of the new association Green and Sustainable Finance Cluster Germany e. V. was not answered even after two requests.

On October 20, 2020, members of the Research Group Finance and Economics of the Global Ethic Institute participated in the public ECB Strategy Review (“The ECB is listening”), and a research group member drew attention to fundamental rights violations with the following text in German language: "By not respecting the EU Charter on Fundamental Rights in its core business (marketable assets, purchase programs, etc.), the ECB's monetary policy actively promotes the expansion of economic practices that do not comply with fundamental rights by financing or assisting in financing them. This is of great concern to me and has therefore been addressed in the form of EU Petition 0429/2017 (Commitment of the European Central Bank to EU Charter on Fundamental Rights). Documentation see here: www.wirtschaftsethik.biz/zentralbank." Thus, the petition has also come to the attention of the strategy review body of the ECB and could have been included in the submission to Ms. Lagarde. Originally, the Research Group Finance and Economics of the Global Ethic Institute would have liked to participate in the live discussion with Ms. Lagarde, but this was not approved.

In an online conversation with the European Policy Centre in November 2020, Christine Lagarde confirmed the legality of the steering option through the selection of marketable assets, which was most likely first brought into play by the petition (see "EPC Thought Leadership Forum with Christine Lagarde" of November 30, 2020, on YouTube https://youtu.be/9_Uc70bC_2U). She referred to the application of the taxonomy for sustainable investments of the EU Commission but proved that she would be able to implement the corrections demanded in the petition immediately on the basis of existing legal foundations—as the EU Charter of Fundamental Rights has already been for 10 years.

Under the umbrella of the New Economics Foundation, the study "GREENING THE EUROSYSTEM COLLATERAL FRAMEWORK—How to decarbonise the ECB's monetary policy" of Yannis Dafermos, Daniela Gabor, Maria Nikolaidi, Adam Pawloff, and Frank van Lerven was published in March 2021. Similar to argumentation in the petition, the study shows that the assets accepted by the European Central Bank as loan collateral contain a disproportionately high number of climate-damaging companies and that these also benefit from lower discounts in the risk assessment.

On April 13, 2021, the environmental protection organization ClientEarth filed its first lawsuit in Belgium against the Belgian central bank, as an example for all central banks of the Eurosystem, in order to stop the central bank's bond purchases as a vicarious agent of the ECB, which are incompatible with the climate goals of the European Union (see http://climatecasechart.com/non-us-case/clientearth-v-belgian-national-bank/). Attached is a request for referral to the European Court of Justice with reference to the EU Charter of Fundamental Rights. ClientEarth explained the background of the lawsuit the day before in a request to Christine Lagarde to finally stop the breaches of law (see https://www.clientearth.org/latest/documents/letter-from-clientearth-to-christine-lagarde-president-of-the-european-central-bank/). The further course of the lawsuit would have been significant for the implementation of the claims of the petition, because all other provisions of the Charter of Fundamental Rights are also actionable and relevant—not only climate protection, which is singled out in that case in isolation. Unfortunatley, ClientEarth announced that it withdrew its case September 2022, because of the new climate risk assessments that the ECB had implemented.

In June 2021, Dr. Roda Verheyen (Judge at the Constitutional Court of Hamburg and co-founder and board member of Green Legal Impact Germany e.V.) published a legal opinion in German language together with Greenpeace, from which the obligation of the ECB to consider climate objectives in its activities emerges. On p. 21 f., the expert opinion also substantiates the ECB's fundamental rights charter obligation (see https://www.greenpeace.de/klimaschutz/zentralbanken-handeln and https://www.greenpeace.de/publikationen/2021-6-09_gutachten_ezb_final_2.pdf) and argues in a comparable way like Marian Szidzek and Dr. jur. Christian Szidzek at the 2019 conference of the Global Ethic Research Group on Finance and Economics, which was published in the volume *The European Central Bank as a Sustainability Role Model* (https://link.springer.com/chapter/10.1007/978-3-030-55450-7_5) p. 43 ff.

In July 2021, the ECB communicated for the first time an "action plan to include climate change considerations in its monetary policy strategy." Some demands of the petition, which had previously been rejected with flimsy arguments, seem to be suddenly being implemented in that plan, but only selectively for climate protection aspects and not for all aspects of the EU Charter of Fundamental Rights. The following plans became particularly relevant (see ECB press release July 8, 2021 https://www.ecb.europa.eu/press/pr/date/2021/html/ecb.pr210708_1~f104919225.en.html):

"Disclosures as a requirement for eligibility as collateral and asset purchases. The ECB will introduce disclosure requirements for private sector assets as a new eligibility criterion or as a basis for a differentiated treatment for collateral and asset purchases. Such requirements will take into account EU policies and initiatives in the field of environmental sustainability disclosure and reporting and will promote more consistent disclosure practices in the market, while maintaining proportionality through adjusted requirements for small and medium-sized enterprises. The ECB will announce a detailed plan in 2022. [. . .] Collateral framework. The ECB will consider relevant climate change risks when reviewing the valuation and risk control frameworks for assets mobilised as collateral by counterparties for Eurosystem credit operations. [. . .] Corporate sector asset purchases. The ECB has already started to take relevant climate change risks into account in its due diligence procedures for its corporate sector asset purchases in its monetary policy portfolios. Looking ahead, the ECB will adjust the framework guiding the allocation of corporate bond purchases to incorporate climate change criteria, in line with its mandate. These will include the alignment of issuers with, at a minimum, EU legislation implementing the Paris agreement through climate change-related metrics or commitments of the issuers to such goals. Furthermore, the ECB will start disclosing climate-related information of the corporate sector purchase programme (CSPP) by the first quarter of 2023 [. . .]."

This proves once again that the ECB is fully aware of its shaping power and its responsibility towards the Charter of Fundamental Rights but only wants to live up to it selectively and al-gusto. Aspects such as child labor (Art. 32), environmental protection even beyond climate risks (Art. 37), or human rights violations (Art. 5) such as forced labor but also tax avoidance and corruption or even the production of outlawed weapons continue to be deliberately ignored. For the first time in history, the fact that market neutrality is neither possible nor necessary is demonstrated by the ECB's own decisions now. The ECB shows herself that monetary policy always has an impact on the real world—also on climate change.

As shown in a press release on the web on March 9, 2022 (see https://insights.issgovernance.com/posts/iss-esg-provides-climate-related-data-and-reporting-under-eurosystem-central-banks-framework-agreement/), ISS ESG provides climate-related data for use within the Eurosystem's central bank framework agreement. With this framework agreement, the ECB refutes once again its own argument that rating assessments by private companies like ISS could not be used by the ECB. In May 2022, the Office of the Committee on Petitions was informed about that by the petitioner, because it might be relevant for the Committee on Legal Affairs, that the ECB is purchasing climate change data about companies from ISS via the Deutsche Bundesbank, thus following the proposal of the 2017 petition.

In January 2022, staff of the ECB responded to a direct citizen inquiry on the core of the petition. The correspondence of the ECB's Directorate General Communication with the citizen is extremely revealing and shows the prevailing understanding of transparency and credibility in the European Central Bank's communication practice on the subject. In October 2021, the citizen asked the ECB Visitor Centre by e-mail in German language to answer the question "Should the ECB deliberately ignore human rights violations and participate in the financing of outlawed weapons and the destruction of the environment and the exploitation of people? Can price stability only be achieved by supporting crime?" The Directorate General of Communications (Internal Communications and Public Affairs) then responded to the citizen in November 2021: "With reference to your questions, we would like to refer to the comments made by ECB President Christine Lagarde in her letter to Clare Daly, Member of the European Parliament: [. . .] Like all EU institutions, the ECB is an addressee of the Charter of Fundamental Rights. The ECB respects the rights, observes the principles and promotes the application thereof, in ac-cordance with its powers and respecting the limits of the powers of the Union as conferred on it in the Treaties. This covers all the ECB's tasks in the fields of monetary policy and banking supervision, in its advisory capacity, as well as its role under the Treaty establishing the Euro-pean Stability Mechanism (ESM) and Regulation (EU) No 472/2013.1. Reviewing the com-patibility of the ECB's actions with the Charter is part of our internal legal scrutiny procedures, which are followed for all actions through which the ECB discharges its tasks. In addition, the conformity of the ECB's actions with the Charter is reviewable by the Court of Justice of the European Union, which has affirmed that the ECB acts in line with the Charter. In this context, I would like to point out that the ECB has a specific mandate and is assigned specific tasks under the Treaties, unlike the Commission, which, as the guardian of the Treaties, is tasked with monitoring the application of EU law in general. The ECB's accountability to the European Parliament provides an additional channel to ensure such compliance."

The citizen replied in January 2022 as follows, referring to the website wirtschaftsethik.biz/zentralbank: "Regarding Ms. Lagarde's quote, the following question: Why are unethical issuers accepted in the 'marketable assets' by the

ECB and no fundamental rights compliance is checked at all, if the Charter applies to 'all the ECB's tasks in the fields of monetary policy'? I would appreciate a response on this. Thank you very much for your efforts." Two days later, the citizen received this sobering reply: "Please understand that the European Central Bank does not comment on media articles or quotes. We therefore have nothing to add to our previous reply." Thereupon, the citizen expressed his understanding and had only asked for an answer to his concrete and simple question without commenting on the "media article": "therefore, I only ask for a simple answer to my concrete question: Why are unethical issuers accepted in the 'marketable assets' by the ECB and no fundamental rights compliance is checked at all, if the Charter applies to 'all the ECB's tasks in the fields of monetary policy'? I would appreciate an answer to this." The ECB's final response to this came 10 days later January 25, 2022—obviously some internal clarification was needed after all: "thank you very much for your e-mail of January 15, 2022. Please understand that we have nothing to add to our reply of January 10, 2022. Yours sincerely."

4 An Interim Conclusion

Even after 4 years, the status was still alarming: protracted, inadequate responses and a large lack of understanding of high decision-makers showed how bad the situation for fundamental rights in the European financial markets still was. Since the last meeting of the EU Committee of Petitions in Brussels 2019 talking about the petition, the following weighty points had developed in the spirit of the petition:

- The ECJ confirmed in a 2019 ruling that "the special status accorded to the ECB in the institutional setup of the Treaties does not exempt it from compliance with the fundamental rights of the Union or from its duty to contribute to the achievement of the Union's objectives as set out in Articles 2, 3 and 6 TEU."
- Another legal opinion on the obligation to take climate protection into account in ECB monetary policy became available, which also refers to the EU Charter of Fundamental Rights.
- Another study demonstrated negative effects in terms of climate protection due to the ECB's collateral policy, thus continuing the revelations of the petition.
- A first lawsuit became pending in Belgium aiming at climate protection and arguing in the spirit of the petition.
- The ECB itself announced a strategy adjustment in climate protection that follows the petition's argumentation and thus itself demonstrated that market neutrality is neither possible nor legally required or even politically expedient.

Some parliamentarians in relevant EU Parliament Committees seemed neither to understand all the presented facts nor their significance, and some still hide behind simple arguments about market neutrality and the ECB's supposedly unlimited independence. Parliamentarians seeking transparency and change became too easily satisfied with inadequate answers from the ECB. The EU Petitions Committee had again been inactive for too long and had once again left the handling of the petition in abeyance for another year. But the president of the ECB as well as the European Commission and all relevant Committees of the European Parliament were demonstrably informed about the problems identified in the petition and options to remedy them. Inaction of all relevant actors can therefore no longer be excused by unknowingness.

5 On the Agenda Again

To get the public discussion going, Weltethos (Global Ethic) Research Group on Finance and Economics was once again organizing another high-profile conference with experts in the field on October 13, 2021, in Frankfurt "Die Europäische Zentralbank und ihre Rolle in einem nachhaltigen Finanzsystem—Probleme und Chancen (The European Central Bank and its role in a sustainable financial system—problems and opportunities)" (see https://www.wirtschaftsethik.biz/vortrag/die-glaubwuerdigkeit-der-ezb-auf-dem-pruefstand-13102021/). The contributions and discussions were mainly in German language, but the conference delegates from the Club of Rome enriched the conference in English language with a global perspective on the role of the ECB in the required worldwide transformation towards sustainability. Directly after that conference, the petition was put back on the agenda of the Petitions Committee on December 1, 2021, on the initiative of MEP Peter Jahr.

5.1 Discussing the Status Quo

On December 1, 2021, the further procedure was discussed in the Committee of Petitions in Brussels after a live statement by Harald J. Bolsinger and Jens Minnemann at 16:45. The Petitions Committee again got an updated speech script, which made the main points as clear as possible in the shortest possible form:

"The Problem: Still unchanged!

ECBs core business does still not take EU Fundamental Rights into account.

- The ECB still seeingly becomes owner of assets that undermine the EU Charter of Fundamental Rights with severe ethical controversies
- All eligible marketable assets (16 trillion € in Q3/2021) and all asset purchases lack the securing of fundamental rights at all!

→ ECB is still part of **financing** fundamental rights violations.

→ This stabilizes and **enhances injustice in the EU**.

Change & Insights: Justice needed!

Int. conference of Global Ethic Institute with the Club of Rome at Goethe University Frankfurt on 13.10.2021

- Latest ECB strategy change shows by climate risk consideration, that ...
  - ... the ECB knows about their power to impact real world actions by strategic assets purchase (there is no such thing like “market neutrality”)
  - ... only a fragment of the whole normative responsibility of the ECB is considered selectively by them.
- The mandate of striving for price stability must not override other EU regulations (e.g., also the Paris Climate Agreement)

„Bring justice into the Eurosystem:
By detailed Transparency to the Parliament.“

Make the ECB report on fundamental rights compliance explicitly of all their assets to the EU Parliament regularly

- You are the Guardians of the Charter of Fundamental Rights: **Please** inform yourself in detail if ECBs assets comply with our codified European values.
- “ECB is accountable for its policies, including through regular reporting and dialogue with the European Parliament (Article 284 TFEU).”

  → **It must become a standard, that the ECB reports on fundamental rights compliance explicitly of all their assets** to the Parliament regularly.

  → This has still never happened before! Is it irrelevant to political decision makers?”

The petitioner underlined the main points in his speech that is reproduced here correspondingly with the most important parts: “The ECB still seeingly becomes owner of assets that undermine the EU Charter of Fundamental Rights with severe ethical controversies. All eligible marketable assets (16 trillion € in Q3/2021) and all asset purchases lack the securing of fundamental rights at all! So ECB is still part of financing fundamental rights violations, and this stabilizes and enhances injustice in the EU. [...] We again held a conference together with our friends of the Club of Rome and the Global Ethic Institute at Frankfurt University—exactly 7 weeks before this meeting today. We have discussed the petition in the light of the current ECB strategy change and a broad international perspective. [...]. It is not only a matter of sustainability ratings for fundamental rights compliance of assets, to go against the glaring injustice of the ECB. It’s a matter of the heart of the decision-makers! They must realize first by themselves that they are ignoring EU’s fundamental rights in their core business! This is the only way for a real and long-lasting change.

The hearts of the ECB board and especially Christine Lagarde seem to have softened a little bit in that respect. They decided to respect climate risk in their daily business in the future. But that is not even half the battle! And what is more—this decision was even not theirs to make! It was, is, and will always be a decision of the EU Parliament, in what framework the ECB must act independently. It is the representatives of the nations and all citizens who have already decided on that.

They decided to make the Charter of Fundamental Rights binding for all European Institutions—including the ECB. Now it's high time for justice—20 years after this decision! The ECB cannot just pick out individual aspects as it sees fit!

We—and the ECB in particular—also need to respect environmental risks as a whole and also health risks, slavery risks, the risk of forced labor and child labor, discrimination risks, social risks, the risk of unfair and unjust working conditions, the risk of corruption and tax avoidance on a large scale, the risk of losing human dignity, the risk to undermine any or all of our fundamental rights, and therefore the perpetuation of injustice all over the European Union. You are the Guardians of the Charter of Fundamental Rights: Please inform yourself in detail if ECB's assets comply with our codified European values. It must become a standard that the ECB reports on fundamental rights compliance explicitly of all their assets to the Parliament regularly. This has still never happened before! We really wish that your hearts also become stirred. This injustice is not only a matter of courts.

In the last monetary dialogue of the Committee on Economic and Monetary Affairs on November 15, 2021, 'The European Parliament considers that improvements to the ECB accountability framework could, and should, be made.' This is the right way! We have to 'paint the dragon red'—we have to make visible what is really going on with ECB's assets to all members of the European Parliament. You can easily make Christine Lagarde report publicly to the European Parliament about the fundamental rights compliance of every single asset owned by the ECB. This is very easy, as I did the same rating by myself 2017 and 2019, and it does not imply any intervention into the independency of the ECB's monetary policy. It is just a detailed report what effects are triggered in the real world with the support of ECB's firepower. This should be published regularly by the ECB—including, but not limited to, climate risk."

After the appeal to the Committee to finally bring justice to the Eurosystem by demanding at least in a first step transparency of the ECB on fundamental rights controversies on all its assets, clear voices were also heard in the Committee:

- The representative of the European Commission underlined the importance of the petition and meanwhile agreed that all EU institutions were bound by the Charter of Fundamental Rights, *but the ECB was alone responsible in the* EU *in* "these things" *and therefore alone the responsible partner. The ECB is responsible and not the commission.* Thus, even under Ursula von der Leyen, the European Commission maintains the opinion that the ECB can simply continue to do whatever it wants regarding the observance of fundamental rights.
- Peter Jahr for the EPP pointed out that independence always has limits that must be precisely balanced—this also would apply to the ECB. However, the experts for the issue of the petition were in the ECON, which is why, in his opinion, that Committee should continue to deal with it. Christine Lagarde should also be asked once again directly to give the ECB's opinion on the petition to the EU Parliament.
- The Vice-President of the Petitions Committee, Yana Toom, active for the Renew Europe Group, brought the bureaucratic handling of the petition to the point: The ECB would quote the answer of the European Commission, and the Commission

in turn would quote itself with the result that the answer would be exhausted in the sense of a "Well, there is nothing we can do!" Ms. Toom does not accept a zero reply to the important question of the petition, which would be passed on like a hot potato for years without any result. Therefore, she asked to keep a special eye on concrete answers and to insist on an answer, for example, from the ECON.

- The President of the Petitions Committee, Dolors Montserrat, finally decided that the petition would not be passed on to the ECON again, as a response had already been received. Only once again a letter should go to the ECB, with a renewed request for opinion by the president.

Peter Jahr's reference to the ECON was correct, but dealing with the issue had already taken place there without any significant follow-up, as the information provided by Gabriele Bischoff already showed. Above all, Ms. Tooms' evaluation encouraged us that the claims of the petition should be discussed nevertheless still seriously with the responsible decision-makers without excuses. The decision of the chairwoman of the Petitions Committee to write to the ECB requesting its opinion seems to be the lowest common denominator of this meeting, on which all hope for justice in the Eurosystem now continues to rest. (The video documentation of the whole meeting is available as a stream here: https://multimedia.europarl.europa.eu/en/event_20211201-1645-COMMITTEE-PETI_vd?start=20211201155114&end=20211201163030).

5.2 *Again: Waiting for Action*

There was still no discernible initiative after the discussion in the Petitions Committee to establish transparency for the European Parliament on the fundamental rights compliance of the ECB's entire assets. But another important action taken was a letter of the Committee to Christine Lagarde, which was sent to the ECON as an imprint, so the ECON can itself launch activities to bring light into the ethical darkness of the ECB's assets. Promptly on December 17, 2021, the chairwoman of the Petitions Committee informed about the letter she has sent directly to Christine Lagarde:

"Vorsitzende des Petitionsausschusses
D 309220 20.12.2021 Brussels, KV/jf[IPOL-COM-PETI D(2021)2861 J]
To the President of the European Central Bank Mrs Christine Lagarde
[...]
Subject: Petition No. 0429/2017 by Harald J. Bolsinger (German) on the compliance of the European Central Bank with the EU Charter of Fundamental Rights

Dear President,

Please be informed that the Committee on Petitions continued to examine petition 0429/2017 in its meeting on 1 December. At the end of the debate, the committee decided to keep the petition open and to forward to you the open letter by the petitioner of 20 October 2020. Please find the letter attached, in which the petitioner requests a personal reply from you as President of the European Central Bank.

We would appreciate any further information and comments you could offer on the matter. Should you require further information, please contact the Secretariat of the Committee on Petitions at [...]

Yours sincerely,

Dolors Montserrat

Chair

Committee on Petitions

Annex: Open letter by the petitioner o/20/10/2020"

The open letter that was in the annex was no longer quite up to date, as the ECB has changed its strategy in the meantime, but we were curious to see whether the ECB's response now includes concrete actions and whether ECON will take up the issue again with the demand for real transparency from the ECB.

In April 2022, the Office of the Committee on Petitions was asked whether the ECB's response was now available. This was not yet the case at that time. However, the Office of the Committee on Petitions informed about forwarding the petition to the Committee on Legal Affairs of the European Parliament in order to have due diligence standards clarified. This indicates that the Committee on Petitions really wanted to answer the petitions' questions deeply and in a finalized way, this time. In September 2022, again the Office of the Committee on Petitions was asked whether the ECB's response was now available at last. This was now the case and the Office of the Committee on Petitions forwarded the reply of the ECB of 21 July 2022 to Ms Dolors Montserrat, again not coming from President Lagarde directly, but only from the deputy directors general of "international and European relations" and "legal services": "Honourable Member of the European Parliament, dear Ms Dolors Montserrat, Thank you for your letter regarding Petition No 0429/2017 on the compliance of the European Central Bank (ECB) with the European Union (EU) Charter of Fundamental Rights (the Charter). The ECB's previous letter replying to this petition, dated 5 August 2020, explained the objectives and the limits established by EU law with regard to the ECB's actions. While reiterating those considerations, in reply to the specific point on sustainability raised by the petitioner, recent developments in ECB policies and actions may merit further clarification. The petitioner refers to statements made by members of the Executive Board—the ECB recognises the urgency and importance of climate change and has committed to actively contributing to efforts at the EU level in this regard. Reflections on climate change and environmental sustainability therefore featured prominently in our monetary policy strategy review of 2020-21. [...] As a result, the Governing Council of the ECB decided on a comprehensive action plan to systematically incorporate climate change considerations into our monetary policy framework, in line with the ECB's mandate. This action plan includes expanding our analytical capacity in macroeconomic modelling, statistics and monetary policy with regard to climate change, as well as incorporating climate change considerations into monetary policy operations in the areas of disclosure, risk assessment, the collateral framework and corporate sector asset purchases. [...] The ECB, together with the Eurosystem, has worked intensely over the last year to deliver on the commitments set out in the action plan. On 4 July 2022, the ECB announced its decision to account for climate change in our corporate bond purchases, collateral framework, disclosure requirements and risk management. The Governing Council has decided to adjust corporate bond holdings in the Eurosystem's monetary policy portfolios, to introduce limits on carbon-intensive corporate assets in its collateral framework, to introduce climate-related disclosure requirements and to enhance its risk management practices in relation to climate change. Corporate bond holdings in the Eurosystem's monetary policy portfolio will be tilted towards issuers with better climate performance, through the reinvestment of the sizeable redemptions expected over the coming years. The share of assets issued by corporate entities with a high carbon footprint that can be pledged as collateral by individual counterparties in Eurosystem credit operations will be limited. Furthermore, for marketable assets and credit claims from companies and debtors subject to the Corporate Sustainability Reporting Directive (CSRD)—once fully implemented—the Eurosystem will only accept them as collateral in Eurosystem credit operations if these entities comply with the CSRD's requirements. The Eurosystem will further enhance its risk assessment tools and capabilities to better include climate-related risks by urging credit rating agencies (CRAs) to be more transparent about how they incorporate climate risks into their ratings and to be more ambitious in their disclosure requirements on climate risks, and through common minimum standards for the inclusion of climate-related risks in national central banks' in-house credit assessment systems. These measures are designed in full accordance with the Eurosystem's primary objective of maintaining price stability. They aim to better take into account climate-related financial risk in the Eurosystem balance sheet and, with reference to our secondary objective, support the green transition of the economy in line with the EU's climate neutrality objectives. Moreover, our measures provide incentives to companies and financial institutions to be more transparent about their carbon emissions and to reduce these emissions. [...] These steps are an example of how the ECB, within the limits of its mandate, is participating in the efforts made by the competent authorities to take action in an important area that is also covered by the Charter. With regard to compliance with the Charter more broadly, the Eurosystem's monetary policy framework is based on clear and transparent rules which are available to Eurosystem counterparties, issuers of Eurosystem eligible collateral, other interested stakeholders and the general public. The principles of an open market economy with free competition, favouring an efficient allocation of resources, proportionality and equal treatment are particularly important in the implementation of the ECB's mandate. On the specific point of the collateral framework referred to by the petitioner, as already explained, the eligibility of assets as collateral for credit operations is primarily guided by considerations regarding the monetary policy objective and appropriate risk management, in order to shield the Eurosystem from potential losses. Ensuring the adequacy of collateral is explicitly required by Article 18.1 of the Statute of the ESCB, which expresses the broader principle of sound management of public finances. The risk management tools include well-established credit assessments produced by accepted external CRAs, alongside other sources. Each accepted CRA must fulfil a number of regulatory and operational requirements and is subject to regular checks by the Eurosystem to dynamically assess its performance in correctly assessing credit risks. Such checks are based on objective (quantitative) data on credit events that provide a basis for statistical tests rather than on broader assessments of the issuer's economic activities. By contrast, no such mechanism exists for ethical or sustainability criteria including those reflecting the Charter, which by their very nature involve broader assessments and balancing acts that go beyond credit risk assessment. Moreover, as mentioned in the previous letter replying to this petition, in line with the principles of institutional balance and the conferral of powers, the ECB cannot replace other authorities responsible for ensuring the compliance of private parties with their legal obligations. In addition, the ECB cannot take action to extend the Charter's scope of application. In summary, to the extent clear and uniform disclosure and reporting obligations exist, the ECB, within the scope of its mandate, will consider them. On precisely this point, the Eurosystem will urge CRAs to be more transparent about how they incorporate climate risks into their ratings and to be more ambitious in their disclosure requirements on climate risks. However, at this stage the precise definition of compliance with the wide-ranging set of legal requirements indicated in the letter from the petitioner can hardly be assessed using the instruments at the disposal of the ECB. An authoritative assessment of such compliance can only be made by the competent authorities, including national and EU courts, which offer specific remedies for potential violations. Hence, the ECB does not see a contradiction between its acceptance of CRAs and the fact that it cannot defer the hypothetical checks of issuers compliance with the Charter to the findings of private selfauthenticated sources such as those proposed by the petitioner. We trust that the above considerations, in addition to those provided in the reply of 5 August 2020, further clarify the ECB's position on the matter and address the concerns raised in the letter from the petitioner. Yours sincerely, [. . .]" The significance of the petition's question at the ECB still does not seem to be high enough, so that the President deems it necessary to respond personally to the petitions committee. In terms of content, the answer remains at the same level as the previous answers. The ECB defends its selective consideration of climate risk and claims that all other risks of systematic undermining of EU fundamental rights do not have to be on its agenda or that it cannot quantify them. At the same time, it paradoxically claims to take them into account as far as necessary. EU fundamental rights violations by companies will not lead to the ECB refusing their bonds as collateral or refusing to purchase them. The ECB summarizes: "An authoritative assessment of such compliance [with the Charter of Fundamental Rights] can only be made by the competent authorities, including national and EU courts, which offer specific remedies for potential violations." With this final sentence the ECB makes clear, that she does not see herself as a "competent authority" that can verify the extent to which potential violations of the Charter of Fundamental Rights have occurred. Rather, the ECB sees courts in the duty doing that. It is a real indictment of a European institution to refer to courts in the year 2022 instead of implementing their own obligation to respect EU fundamental rights in all its actions—including in monetary policy instruments, which should have happened since 1999. After this answer and the course of the petition so far it seems obvious that the ECB will only take care of this problem when sued before the ECJ or if the EU Commission and the EU Parliament intervene politically in another strong way.

6 Questions and Outlook

Jens Minnemann gives an overview about credibility in the financial market in a practical perspective in this book (see Chapter "Credibility in the Financial Market: A Practical Perspective"). Against the background of his aspects and the answers that the ECB gave in the context of this petition, the credibility of the ECB appears to be fraught with many questions:

1. Focus on core mission and core competence (expertness): There seems to be a political and scientific controversy about the objectives and the scope for monetary actions of the ECB—although the European treaties including the Charter of Fundamental Rights have clear answers to that already! Does the ECB know what its core mandate really is and within what limiting values framework this may be pursued? Is the ECB an ethical blind technocrat for price stability in the Eurozone, or is it a values-bound European institution among other European institutions that serve the European people with values-led monetary policy?
2. Honest and clear communication (trustworthiness): Is there real transparency about the whole impact of monetary policy decisions, or do the decision makers obfuscate real-world impact of their actions? What data must the ECB collect, check, and report to minimize negative impacts on European core values codified in the Charter of Fundamental Rights? Who must assess the reports and discuss them politically?
3. Alignment with the needs of the customer (expertness): Who must the ECB serve and how exactly? The EU Parliament, European nations, the population, financial market actors, etc.?
4. Fair (fairness): Is it fair to invest in injustice by ignoring real-world impact and violations of fundamental rights? Can the ECB be a role model for commercial banks, or is it ok to demand from them something that the ECB does not deliver herself? Are there trade-offs or red lines between "market neutrality" and EU values?
5. Compliance with legal requirements and framework conditions (trustworthiness): What about the European treaties? Is the ECB above the EU Fundamental Rights Charter? What are the limits of ECB's independence? Who must enforce fundamental rights compliance of monetary policy?

Summing up the experienced up to now, there is still a real opportunity to politically counter the Eurosystem's ethical blindness in the current election period. Even when one could gain the impression that there would be a political blanket of silence on the petition since the beginning in 2017, it gives hope that the Committee on Petitions has put the petition on the agenda again at the end of 2021 and is still assessing the answers of the ECB.

It remains a central question for the credibility of the EU Charter of Fundamental Rights of the European Union how this petition ends and with what justifications for action or no action. The EU Commission and the relevant EU Parliament Committees are still not positioned in a clear way what weight and role the Charter of Fundamental Rights of the European Union has in European financial markets. The same can be said also for the credibility of the ECB. As it was made clear in this article, there is still a discussion about a hypothetical controversy and about an alleged problem of priorities. It is the shade discussion about a nowhere derivable unlimited independence of the ECB and about the supposed conflict of objectives between sustainability and price stability. The solution to all existing and future conflicts exists! It is the simple conformity to fundamental rights as guardrails in every decision of every European institution. Credible is who really respects fundamental rights and protects them in all aspects of his business, instead of discussing the limits of the charter for ages!

References

Bolsinger H (2021) Fundamental rights in the core business of the ECB: no issue?! - experience with the EU petition 429/2017. In: Bolsinger H, Hoffmann J, Villhauer B (eds) The European Central Bank as a sustainability role model – philosophical, ethical and economic perspectives. Springer, p 19 ff

Szidzek M (2021) Legal approaches to encouraging the ECB to comply with human rights aspects when establishing the list of marketable assets. In: Bolsinger H, Hoffmann J, Villhauer B (eds) The European Central Bank as a sustainability role model – philosophical, ethical and economic perspectives. Springer, p 43 ff

Web Links

http://climatecasechart.com/non-us-case/clientearth-v-belgian-national-bank/. Accessed 27 Dec 2022

https://www.clientearth.org/latest/documents/letter-from-clientearth-to-christine-lagarde-president-of-the-european-central-bank/. Accessed 31 May 2022

https://www.ecb.europa.eu/paym/coll/charts/html/index.en.html. Accessed 31 May 2022

https://www.ecb.europa.eu/pub/pdf/other/ecb.mepletter200619_Daly~cee67c7de1.en.pdf. Accessed 31 May 2022

https://www.ecb.europa.eu/press/pr/date/2021/html/ecb.pr210708_1~f104919225.en.html. Accessed 31 May 2022

https://ec.europa.eu/info/sites/default/files/political-guidelines-next-commission_en_0.pdf. Accessed 31 May 2022

https://eur-lex.europa.eu/legal-content/EN/TXT/?uri=CELEX:62017TJ0107. Accessed 31 May 2022

https://www.greenpeace.de/klimaschutz/zentralbanken-handeln. Accessed 31 May 2022

https://www.greenpeace.de/publikationen/2021-6-09_gutachten_ezb_final_2.pdf. Accessed 31 May 2022

https://www.greenpeace.de/sites/default/files/media_type_pdf/2021_05_studie_greening_the_eurosystem_collateral_framework-report-ENG.pdf. Accessed 30 April 2022
https://insights.issgovernance.com/posts/iss-esg-provides-climate-related-data-and-reporting-under-eurosystem-central-banks-framework-agreement/. Accessed 31 May 2022
https://www.nachhaltigkeitsrat.de/wp-content/uploads/2019/10/2019-10-15_Stellungnahme_Sustainable_Finance_Strategie_der_Bundesregierung.pdf. Accessed 31 May 2022
https://www.wirtschaftsethik.biz/centralbank. Accessed 31 May 2022
https://www.wirtschaftsethik.biz/vortrag/die-glaubwuerdigkeit-der-ezb-auf-dem-pruefstand-13102021/. Accessed 31 May 2022
https://www.wirtschaftsethik.biz/Zentralbank. Accessed 31 May 2022

Video Sources

https://www.europarl.europa.eu/streaming/?event=20191111-1500-COMMITTEE-PETI&start=2019-11-11T14:08:49Z&end=2019-11-11T16:29:36Z&language=en. Accessed 27 Dec 2022
https://multimedia.europarl.europa.eu/en/event_20211201-1645-COMMITTEE-PETI_vd?start=20211201155114&end=20211201163030. Accessed 27 Dec 2022
https://www.tagesschau.de/multimedia/video/video-628293.html. Accessed 27 Dec 2022
https://youtu.be/9_Uc70bC_2U. "EPC thought leadership forum with Christine Lagarde", 30.11.2020. Accessed 27 Dec 2022

What to Do with Modern Money Theory (MMT)?

von Dirk Ehnts

Abstract What impact does Modern Money Theory (MMT) have on the different dynamics toward a new (European) strategy of sustainability? The paper discusses the impact on the public, policy makers, central bankers, academics (both economists and noneconomists), and students of economics. Being an empirical monetary theory, MMT cannot be "applied", but builds on existing institutions. All recommendations are easi to implement. That makes the MMT, Ehnts argues, a powerful instrument to address the problems of our day.

1 Introduction

The COVID-19 pandemic has led policy makers and academics to rethink the role of the state (Mazzucato 2021). Ideas about economic policy have changed dramatically. In the Eurozone, the pandemic caused many societies to institute a lockdown, which created an economic recession. Tax revenues fell as production plummeted. In Germany, calls for austerity policy—cuts in government spending and the occasional rise in tax rates—and a lower interest rate set by the ECB would have been a continuation of the economic policy regime in the first half of the 2010s. Rather, policy makers turned to a large increase in government spending to pay workers' wages to stop them from becoming unemployed. Furlough and job retention schemes were the rule rather than the exception, with the USA being the only larger country not to support workers' incomes in this way. Instead, stimulus checks were sent by the Biden administration to get the economy going after unemployment went up during the first half of 2020.

In Germany, the public bank Kreditanstalt für Wiederaufbau (Bank for Reconstruction) was asked by the finance minister to extend "unlimited loans" in order to save businesses from running out of money during the lockdown. No German

von Dirk Ehnts (✉)
Berlin, Germany
e-mail: dirk@ehnts.de

H. J. Bolsinger et al. (eds.), *The European Central Bank and Its Role in a Sustainable Finance System*, Sustainable Finance, https://doi.org/10.1007/978-3-031-24478-0_7

political party called for the combination of fiscal and monetary policy that had ruled in the Eurocrisis. The government of Greece, with public debt to GDP peaking at around 210% of GDP—compared to 130% of GDP at the start of the Eurocrisis—had no problems at all with executing its payments because the European policy makers acted fast. They threw out the rulebook in March 2020 already, as Ehnts and Paetz (2021a, 2021b) noted. The ECB promised to buy up 750 billion euros worth of financial assets, including government bonds. Meanwhile, the general escape clause of the Stability and Growth Pact was activated so that the deficit limits were off as well. Christine Lagarde stated in November 2020: "As the sole issuer of euro-denominated central bank money, the Eurosystem will always be able to generate additional liquidity as needed. So, by the definition, it will neither go bankrupt nor run out of money."

We are living in a different world now. What has changed is not the reality but the way we look at it. We have realized that governments apparently cannot run out of their own currency and that if only the European policy makers support the Greek government, no debt default is necessary—never mind the interest and growth rate. We have also realized that monetary policy does not work. Woodford (2022) has thrown in the towel for the New Keynesians, stating that monetary policy would not work because it would not create the right kind of aggregate demand—which fiscal policy can create. Understanding the world we are living in is what science is for. Economic science specifically should deal with the economic world, but most modern economic textbooks are not able to explain the empirical phenomena that we have seen in the last years. They are full of discussions of public debt sustainability, of trade-offs between inflation and unemployment rate, and of banks that act as intermediaries to funnel saving(s) toward investments. Galbraith (2004) wrote his book about *The Economics of Innocent Fraud* - the idea that shifting the interest rate would somehow change the rate of inflation was one of them.

Criticizing existing theories is one issue, coming up with a new paradigm to understand the world is a completely different matter. Modern Monetary Theory provides such a lens, applying balance sheets and logic to current and historical monetary systems. Its method is double-entry bookkeeping and equilibrium always rules: the balances balance. The perhaps irritating fact is that MMT is an empirical theory. Its conclusions can be falsified, which sets it apart from all other macroeconomic schools. Summarized in one statement, the MMT approach can be best described like this:

$$\text{macroeconomics} = \text{accounting} + \text{behavior}$$

MMT deals with the accounting part. This is why the core of MMT is not a set of assumptions, like in most other schools. It is a pair of lenses (Ehnts 2022b). The left one is for the assets and the right one for liabilities. Wearing those lenses does force one to see balances. Whether the view is helpful or not depends on the question one is examining. It would be strange, however, to say that MMT would be "wrong." It is a method rather than a model or a set of assumptions, so in what sense can MMT be "wrong"?

For more than a hundred years macroeconomists have debated their ideas by pointing out flaws in the opponents' assumptions or use of units or variables. The Keynesians were attacked because their aggregate consumption function would be too simplistic, the monetarists, because it was not clear what exactly the "money supply" is. How would anyone who has been involved in these debates approach MMT? The obvious route to attack MMT would be to point out flaws, but since there are very little assumptions and much relies on national income and product accounts, there is a problem. MMT scholars do not engage in building macroeconomic models used to predict the future, as other authors did. It is not that there are no such models—there are (Ehnts 2014), and they can easily be calibrated and used to make predictions. It is just that the core of MMT does not include beliefs about certain variables or parameters that macroeconomists have discussed so often. So, what to do with MMT?

2 MMT and the Public

What would the public do with MMT? The monetary system is created by political actions, through laws enacted in parliaments. It is therefore subject to democratic debate. Feinig (2022) points out that there used to be lots of public debates about the monetary system in the US before "monetary silencing" set in. However, the monetary system is a central part of any functioning democracy. As MMT makes clear, money is best understood by looking at the actions of the currency issuer first. Only then should we look at money from the perspective of users of money. This means that money is first of all the instrument of the government to provision itself. It has a public purpose, and in order to execute its functions, the government needs resources. What it wants from the public, its citizens, are labor services, goods and services, and financial and other real assets like real estate. It does not want our money—as the currency issuer, it has a monopoly on money creation and can create as much of it as it wants. What it cannot create are resources.

The public should therefore understand that what the government wants from the private sector (households and firms) is not its money but its resources. Resources are limited, and what the government uses cannot be used by the private sector. Opportunity costs are at the center of the economic argument about who gets which resources. If what the public sector can deliver using a specific set of resources leads to better results than what the private sector can deliver, then there should be no problem for the government to spend its money to acquire those resources. What the private sector loses in terms of resources it gains in (state) money. Given its nature as a tax credit, there is no such thing as "government debt." The debt of the government when issuing currency is that it promises to take back its money for payments to itself. That is hardly what we think about as a "debt." After all, cinemas are not required to publish numbers about the outstanding number of cinema tickets and then divide that number by the yearly sales to create "cinema debt."

It is important that the public understands the correct sequence of money creation:

1. State spends money into the economy.
2. Private sector pays taxes and buys bonds with that money.

A federal government does not "finance" its spending. It creates money when it spends. Kelton (2020) calls this financing by money creation. In the Eurozone, this happens when the national central banks mark up the account of a receiving bank. In turn, the bank marks up the account of the household or firm receiving the payment from the government. There are only two ways to create money in the Eurozone: ECB and national central banks, which form the Eurosystem, must create that money in the interplay with the banking system or the national governments must spend it into existence. At the core, government spending is a monetary operation. Outlawing "monetary financing" in the Eurozone is about as realistic as outlawing "liquidity drinking." There is no practical alternative to governments when they spend.

It would be a disaster for a democracy to replace its domestic currency (or its supranational one) with a foreign currency or bitcoin. This would force the national government to finance its spending, as it would be relegated to currency user. Before spending dollars, a non-US government first has to receive dollars. Before spending bitcoin, a government would first have to receive bitcoin. In such a monetary system, tax revenues and bond revenues would take place before government spending. The sovereignty of the state would be harmed as it could not spend as it wished. In a democracy, government spending is a crucial process. When the budget is passed, the government should be able to spend. To force a government to finance its spending impairs the democratic process. A reduction in government spending could lead to macroeconomic problems like mass unemployment, deflation, and a disruption of international trade.

3 MMT and Policy Makers

Policy makers cannot decide to "apply" MMT or "do" MMT. There are no "MMT policies" that MMT calls for. What MMT does argue is that the federal government targets the public purpose when it spends (Ehnts and Höfgen 2020). What the public purpose is will be defined through the political process. In the end, the federal government picks its preferred set of policies and uses its money to provision itself. MMT argues that the level of government spending should be targeted to achieve full employment and price stability. Once it is understood that the economy is limited by resources and not by deficit or sustainability of public debt, it is clear that the federal government is responsible for the unemployment rate. Given some desired saving by its citizens, the federal government adjusts taxes and tax rates as well as its level of spending to achieve a net injection of money that is compatible with full employment and price stability. Since price stability depends on resource use in a variety of sectors, spending needs to be targeted in a way that takes into account its effect on the price level and inflation.

Policy makers have relied on MMT in the past, even though it's not generally acknowledged. The idea that the central bank should act as a dealer of last resort for government bonds in order to ensure that the federal government is always liquid, and solvent has been taken up in practice by the ECB (Ehnts 2016). Also, ECB presidents like Mario Draghi and Christine Lagarde have been calling to examine MMT. What matters to policy makers is not the history of economic thought or academic debates between different schools but results. What works in practice is preferred to what works in theory, at least in the medium term. The rule of the theory of expansionary austerity, for instance, was very brief, because its results were disastrous. Policy makers today shy away from arguments brought forward a decade ago about the right level of the public debt to GDP ratio and other ideas. They also shy away from using monetary policy as it is well understood that further cuts to the ECB's interest rates would only serve to enrage voters which would then be forced to pay interest on their bank deposits. They have been looking for theoretical alternatives, and MMT provides them with new ideas and framing to find and explain policy solutions to real-world problems. The Biden administration, for instance, features John Yarmouth of Kentucky, who has explained public deficit and debt on C-SPAN using MMT frames (Ehnts 2022a, 6).

Policy makers have turned toward MMT in search for answers to policy problems, and they will continue to do so as the results from established economic theories have disappointed again and again. Inflation targeting does not work to steer inflation and the economy, fiscal sustainability does not even exist, financial markets do not "finance" investment (banks and the central bank do that), and minimum wages do not create unemployment. Economists are by now widely perceived as one-trick ponies: they offer market solutions to any problem offered to them in the name of efficiency (Appelbaum 2019). The vigor of mathematical models has fooled many people a long time, but it seems that this effect is now wearing off. Also, McLeay (2014) has exposed the links between billionaires and the theory of public choice, taking away the reputation of economics as a discipline that is not "political." MMT restores faith in the scientific dimension of economics as its theories are easily understood and do not require scholars to spend much effort to understand MMT. There is a wide variety of free online resources available, including dozens of hours of video.

4 MMT and Academics (Noneconomists)

Other disciplines have been quick to understand MMT and connect it with other fields. Desan (2015) writes about money from a legal perspective, Wullweber (2021) examines central banking from a political perspective, and Sahr (2022) writes about the monetary system from a sociologist's perspective. Given that other academic disciplines are more open, it can be expected that MMT will thrive there. Some of the most important research of the coming years can be expected to come from authors outside of the economics discipline, writing about money and some special issue or question of interdisciplinary character.

MMT itself relies on other academic disciplines as arrangements of debt are not self-explanatory but need to be examined in terms of social structure and ideas of society (Atwood 2008). The creation of states, of central banks, and of ministries of finance is very interesting, but can't be examined using MMT alone. MMT is hence more and more integrated into the wider social science literature. Much can be learned from reinterpretations of the past using MMT. There is a lack of economic history that deals with milestones, like the Great Depression, the stagflation of the 1970s, or the global financial crisis of 2008/2009. Also, a thorough examination of the rise of welfare states in the post-WWII period is still missing. This is a result of the purge of the disciplines of economic history and history of economic thought in universities worldwide. If we want to regain a better understanding of our past, these processes need to be reversed.

Looking forward, the most fruitful cooperation can be expected when those looking for solutions to stop climate change connect with MMT (Olk et al. 2022). The usual assumptions in principles of economics textbooks are that the (microeconomics) supply curve has no end while the monetary supply (macroeconomics) is fixed. While these results have been more and more reversed in mainstream teaching in the last decades, the discipline still seems decades away from realizing that money is available in unlimited quantities, whereas resources are not. MMT leads to a major rethinking of the way we conceptualize the economy and its limits. This gives hope to those trying to find ways to create a sustainable economy with strong democratic roots.

5 MMT and Economists

Broadly, we can divide the economists into three camps. There are those which use MMT as their main focal point, there are post-Keynesians, and there is the mainstream. Post-Keynesian can be divided into those that understand and acknowledge MMT, like Marc Lavoie, Robert Skidelsky, Louis-Philippe Rochon, or Steve Keen, and those who don't (Keen 2021). There is not much to be said about these groups. Post-Keynesian economics as a school covers a far wider range of subjects than MMT currently does. There is much overlap with MMT, and one is left to wonder why post-Keynesian thought mostly ignored sectoral balances, chartalism, and functional finance. If these building blocks were given a more prominent role in post-Keynesian thought, a synthesis around MMT as the core monetary theory could easily be built. Time will tell whether this is the future of economic theory.

Mainstream economists usually don't know what to do with MMT. It must seem alien to them as it is an empirical theory, producing falsifiable statements. Here is one: When a federal government spends, banks see their reserves increase, which causes them to offer these reserves on the interbank market, causing the interest rate to drop. They have complained that there are no mathematical models, which is not true. The problem is that the mathematical models are relying on accounting relationships and stay rather silent on behavior or assume behavior that cannot be easily criticized. MMT does not rely on modeling tricks and assumptions to produce certain results. Assuming that MMT scholars have tried to create intellectual tricks to arrive at pre-agreed practical policy solutions, many authors have looked hard to find out how this has been done. The problem is that they won't find anything because MMT is a descriptive theory and not a package of economic policy recommendations. It explains why we should not expect the central banks' set of interest rates to have a large influence on the economy, and it explains why we should think that government spending has more direct influence.

The methodology to arrive at these conclusions is the macroeconomic accounting with the use of balance sheets that is at the core of MMT. MMT does not claim that other lenses cannot provide important insights. It does not claim that you cannot combine the MMT lens with other lenses. However, it claims that the MMT lens will lead to insights when it comes to money creation and destruction that matter. It is almost impossible to reproduce these results using mainstream models like those developed in Woodford (2003). The whole mindset of the economists working in these two camps is completely different. New Keynesians start with theory and then look at the real world, never doubting their models. MMT scholars start with empirical phenomena and then use accounting to describe the real world. They move from balance sheets of single units to sectoral balances, which aggregates these into the private, public, and external sector. New Keynesians don't think like this at all, using a representative agent or a bunch of heterogeneous agents instead.

Therefore, there is little that MMT scholars can learn from New Keynesians, and there is little that New Keynesians want to learn from MMT scholars. Relying on mathematical modeling, they find nothing that they could use for their elaborate models. When they do, the results are usually disappointing for MMT scholars, as Eggertsson and Krugman (2012) proved. Krugman (2021) writes about the US economy:

At a fundamental level, households are financing the deficit: The funds being borrowed by the government are coming out of the huge savings undertaken by families saving much of their income in an environment where much of their usual consumption hasn't felt safe.

From the MMT perspective, this is like saying that a motor engine inhales fumes and produces gas and air. Krugman gets the sequence completely wrong, claiming that the federal government borrows from household saving (not savings, as Krugman writes) "at a fundamental level." This is completely at odds with the idea that the Fed is the currency issuer. Households need dollars to pay taxes, but the federal government does not need dollars to spend. Krugman is unable to talk about the economics from a monetary perspective.

The future of economics most likely to happen seems to be a paradigm built on MMT, doughnut economics (Raworth 2017), and the mission economy (Mazzucato 2021). There are now groups of MMT and degrowth scholars working on a synthesis. Ryan-Collins et al. (2022) have presented an MMT view of the British monetary system. The academic work is dealing with real-world questions that are important to policy makers. How can we pay for the socio-ecological transformation? How can we create a better economy for everyone? How can we reduce the inequality of wealth and income that threatens our societies? How can we thrive with less material consumption? How can we reform finance so that it serves society instead of the other way around? The answer that mainstream economists have for all these problems is that we should rely on changing incentives and give more power to markets or create new ones. This, however, is what has at least partly caused the big problems of climate change and inequality of income and wealth.

6 MMT and Central Bankers

Drumetz and Pfister (2021), two authors affiliated with the Banque de France, have also addressed MMT. Ehnts (2022a) has replied to the (mis-)reading of what constitutes MMT. Both Christine Lagarde and Mario Draghi mentioned MMT in the press, and not in negative light. What central bankers can do with MMT is quite clear. They can use it to educate the public. How is money created? It took decades until the Bank of England (McLeay et al. 2014) and Deutsche Bundesbank (2017) finally came clear. Bank loans and bank deposits are created simultaneously. Saving or reserves do not and cannot finance bank loans and hence private investment. Both articles explain money creation as transactions, with balance sheets drawn to illustrate the mechanics of it. This seems to be the way forward. The article by Bundesbank also described that money is created when goods and services are exported. The only thing missing now is the creation of money when the government spends. Drumetz and Pfister in private emails promised to reply to Ehnts (2022a), where he challenges the authors to either falsify his balance sheets of money creation by government spending in Germany or provide the equivalent for the case of the French government.

Central bankers have recently lost their paradigm, as Woodford (2022) states that "interest-rate policy cannot eliminate the [macroeconomics] distortions—not because of a limit on the extent to which interest rates can be reduced, but because interest-rate reductions fail to stimulate demand of the right sorts." The New Keynesian compass has failed the central banks, and MMT provides a new compass. Central bankers should not be scared by the critiques of MMT that mainstream academics have written up. Interest rates and monetary policy have had their day, and the last ten years have shown that fiscal policy is more important than monetary policy. In the Eurozone, fiscal austerity overpowered zero interest rates to deliver depression-era outcomes in Greece and Italy. Nowhere, not even in the Eurozone, did low-interest rates and high levels of public debt lead to government default as long as the government uses its own currency. That is why MMT does not argue that central banks should engage in "monetary financing" of governments or that central banks should lose their independence.

MMT does argue that we should aim economic policy at the goals of full employment and price stability. Also, the economy should be sustainable. The Job

Guarantee (JG) is one piece of the puzzle, leading to "true" full employment. However, macroeconomic policies should ensure that there are only very few people in the JG program as it is a direct result of a lack of aggregate demand. Central banks right now have one instrument—the set of interest rates—and one or more goals. It seems that they cannot even hit the price stability target without help from the government. MMT helps central banks to realistically redefine their role as the bank of the state and the liquidity provider for the private banking system. Central banks can stabilize the interest rate and at the same time deliver any amount of net government spending. Therefore, it is rather useless to talk about "fiscal dominance" and "monetary dominance". Central banks do not have to care about the sustainability of public debt—there is no such thing unless the government sells a significant number of bonds in foreign currency.

On a more practical level, MMT can be used to justify central bank purchases of government bonds. These operations ensure that there is enough demand to support the government bonds as a risk-free asset. Its yield over the range of maturities is an important price; hence, the central bank can and must engage in purchases of government bonds if the private sector as a whole wants to unload a significant share of its portfolio. Quantitative easing should be given up, though, as well as the net purchases of private sector assets as a whole as these has no clearly defined policy target. They might drive financial asset prices up, which is an unwanted effect.

7 MMT and Economics Students

Economics students have a lot to gain from MMT. They can learn about money creation and destruction using methods that are not ideological. Examining balance sheets and transactions, they will learn how to move from microeconomics of the household and firm to sectoral balances and the macroeconomic effects of government spending, taxation, and private saving. This hopefully revives interest in the academic study of economics and provides training for the future generation of public servants dealing with economic problems. Those arguing in favor of more pluralist economics can use MMT as a method to compare different macroeconomic schools.

Obviously, MMT structures the macroeconomic questions in a new way, which provides a lot of space for new research. Questions of international trade and development, exchange rate regime choice, and international institutions can be revisited. The same goes for economic history: the Great Depression, the golden era of capitalism in the postwar era, the end of the Bretton Woods system, and the global financial crisis—there are plenty of issues where new insights can be expected. This should go hand in hand with a return of history of economic thought and economic history, as students should be made aware that economic theories are connected to specific problems and situations of power in time.

In terms of graphical models, there are mathematical models like Ehnts (2014) which can be used for teaching at bachelor level and higher. Mitchell et al. (2019) have published a 600-page textbook which can be used for master level or higher as it is very comprehensive. MMT can also serve as a base to master stock-flow consistent models as introduced by Godley and Lavoie (2006). This does not mean that macroeconomic modeling with the equilibrium at its center should be revived, though. Post-Keynesians have stressed (steady state) equilibrium too much, embracing the idea that such a concept has a meaning in the real world. MMT scholars are interested in showing that monetary flows are "in equilibrium" at all times, when accounted for properly. That the economy could come to a rest is a metaphor that should not be used in the twenty-first century. It is incompatible with the idea of a transformation of the economy that is at the center of economic policy for the next decades.

8 Conclusion

What to do with Modern Monetary Theory (MMT)? In this article, I have discussed the impact that MMT has and might have for different groups, namely, the public, policy makers, central bankers, academics (both economists and noneconomists), and students of economics. Of course, the future is unknown, so these ideas should not be mistaken for a path that we should walk together. With MMT, we can hope to overcome the ideologies of the twentieth century and rebuild economics on strong foundations. MMT, after all, is an empirical monetary theory. Its insights can be falsified, which means that MMT is open to change. It is very easy to achieve this change. Anyone could create balance sheets and then describe which transactions are happening when banks create loans, governments spend, central banks buy assets, etc. There are no behavioral assumptions hardwired into MMT. Macroeconomics is accounting plus behavior, but MMT is mostly agnostic about behavior. This, I believe, is a strength of it, not a weakness.

Since monetary policy cannot and will not stimulate the economy, we are at a crossroads. MMT can help to transition into a new era of macroeconomic policy-making, one in which supply and demand are thought together as the strain on the planet's resources becomes more visible by the day. We need to answer different questions from those of half a century ago. That is why we need new theory that allows us to focus on the problems of our day. This does not mean that we should forget the old answers—they are still relevant for the old problems. But every generation has the right to fix its own problems, creating new problems for the next generation. There is no hope to reach a general equilibrium in a dynamic world full of non-stochastic randomness and unintended consequences of large dimensions. The best we can hope for is to deal with the problems of our time.

References

Appelbaum (2019) The Economists' hour: false prophets, free markets, and the fracture of society. Little, Brown and Company

Atwood M (2008) Payback: debt and the shadow side of wealth. Bloomsbury

Desan C (2015) Making money: coin, currency, and the coming of capitalism. Oxford University Press, Oxford

Deutsche Bundesbank (2017) Die Rolle von Banken, Nichtbanken und Zentralbank im Geldschöpfungsprozess, Monatsbericht April 2017, pp 15–36

Drumetz F, Pfister C (2021) Modern monetary theory: a wrong compass for decision-making. Intereconomics 56(6):355–361

Eggertsson GB, Krugman P (2012) Debt, deleveraging, and the liquidity trap: a fisher-Minsky-Koo approach. Q J Econ 127(3):1469–1513

Ehnts D (2014) A simple macroeconomic model of a currency union with endogenous money and saving-investment imbalances. Int J Plur Econ Educ 5(3):279–297

Ehnts D (2016) Modern monetary theory and European macroeconomics. Routledge

Ehnts D (2022a) Modern monetary theory: the right compass for decision-making. Intereconomics 57(2):128–134

Ehnts D (2022b) Modern monetary theory: Eine Einführung. Springer

Ehnts D, Höfgen M (2020) Modern monetary theory and the public purpose. Am Rev Political Econ 15(1): 1–12. https://arpejournal.com/article/id/173/

Ehnts D, Paetz M (2021a) COVID-19 and its economic consequences for the euro area. Eurasian Econ Rev 11:227–249

Ehnts, D, Paetz M (2021b) Wie finanzieren wir die Corona-Schulden? Versuch einer „richtigen“ Antwort auf eine „falsche“ Frage aus Sicht der Modern Monetary Theory. Wirtschaftsdienst 101(6): 200–206

Feinig J (2022) Moral economies of money: politics and the monetary constitution of society. Stanford University Press

Galbraith JK (2004) The economics of innocent fraud: truth for our time. Mariner Books

Godley and Lavoie (2006) Monetary economics: an integrated approach to credit, money, income, production and wealth. Palgrave Macmillan

Keen S (2021) The new economics: a manifesto. Polity

Kelton S (2020) The deficit myth: modern monetary theory and the birth of the People's economy. Public Affairs

Krugman P (2021) Krugman wonks out: what we talk about when we talk about money. https://www.nytimes.com/2021/05/21/opinion/money-federal-reserve-deficit.html

Mazzucato M (2021) Mission economy: a moonshot guide to changing capitalism. Allen Lane

McLeay M, Radia A, Thomas R (2014) Money creation in the modern economy. Bank England Q Bull Q1:14–27

Mitchell W, Watts M, Wray R (2019) Macroeconomics. Bloomsbury Academic

Olk C, Schneider C, Hickel J (2022) How to pay for saving the world: modern monetary theory for a degrowth transition. SSRN Electron J. https://doi.org/10.2139/ssrn.4172005

Raworth K (2017) Doughnut economics: seven ways to think like a 21st-century economist. Cornerstone Digital

Ryan-Collins J, Berkeley A, Tye R, Voldsgaard A, Wilson N (2022) The self-financing state: An institutional analysis of government expenditure, revenue collection and debt issuance operations in the United Kingdom, IIPP working paper 2022/08

Sahr A (2022) Die monetäre Maschine: Eine Kritik der finanziellen Vernunft. C.H. Beck
Woodford M (2003) Interest and prices: foundations of a theory of monetary policy. Princeton University Press
Woodford M (2022) Effective demand failures and the limits of monetary stabilization policy. Am Econ Rev 112(5):1475–1521
Wullweber J (2021) Zentralbankkapitalismus: Transformationen des globalen Finanzsystems in Krisenzeiten. Suhrkamp

The Role of the EU Taxonomy

Bernd Villhauer

Abstract The text describes the relation between the new EU taxonomy and the sustainability activities of the European Central Bank (ECB). These relations are important in order to adequately understand and describe the challenges for a future-proof ECB policy. It gives a short summary of the taxonomy and outlines the essential fields of mutual interaction.

Why is the taxonomy of the European Union important for the ECB's role in a sustainable economy? For a better understanding of the role of this taxonomy, it is important to know why we need a clear definition of sustainability in financial markets.

Because it is precisely the lack of clarity about what sustainability means and can mean—especially from the perspective of investors—that ensures that the European Community has decided to publish a uniform taxonomy. The taxonomy is intended to provide conceptual clarity, without which no reliable investment policy is possible.

To help us understand this better, I will explain what this taxonomy actually entails and for what purpose it is being developed. Then I highlight the effects on the discussion about the ECB to finally describe for future development how taxonomic definitions and strategic orientation of the ECB support each other.

1 Historical Background

In 2016, the EU Commission established a High-Level Expert Group to make suggestions for a strategy to fully integrate sustainability into Europe's system of financial regulation. The group of 20 experts from the finance sector, civil society,

B. Villhauer (✉)
Weltethos-Institut, University of Tübingen, Tübingen, Germany
e-mail: villhauer@weltethos-institut.org

H. J. Bolsinger et al. (eds.), *The European Central Bank and Its Role in a Sustainable Finance System*, Sustainable Finance, https://doi.org/10.1007/978-3-031-24478-0_8

and academy laid out a plan defining what is sustainable and what is not "green," innovative industries or transition technologies. The EU taxonomy was described as a classification system, aiming at establishing a list and description of environmentally sustainable economic activities.

The "Action Plan for Financing Sustainable Growth," now enshrined in EU directives, addresses three main topics:

- Reorienting capital flows toward sustainable investment, in order to achieve sustainable and inclusive growth
- Mainstreaming sustainability into risk management
- Fostering transparency and long-termism in financial and economic activity

It proposes a clear-cut taxonomy as a standardized framework to facilitate sustainable investments. The Action Plan thereby also creates a unified classification system on what can be considered environmentally sustainable economic activities.

Accordingly, the EU creates two new benchmarks to guide investors:

- The low-carbon benchmark
- The positive carbon impact benchmark to be 2 °C compliant

The EU Commission is also taking measures to improve the efficiency and the impact of instruments aimed at sustainable investments in the EU.

A main factor for this is the European Fund for Strategic Investments (EFSI) (since 2021: InvestEU Programme) an initiative of EIB Group and the European Commission aimed at boosting the economy through mobilizing private financing for strategic investments. EFSI was established in 2015 through an EU Regulation 2015/1017 of the European Parliament and of the Council of 25 June 2015 on the European Fund for Strategic Investments, the European Investment Advisory Hub, and the European Investment Project Portal and amending Regulations (EU) No. 1291/2013 and (EU) No. 1316/2013. The EFSI, also known as Juncker Plan, will have an even greater focus on sustainable investments and climate action projects.[1]

The Commission invites the European Securities and Markets Authority (ESMA) to collect information on undue short-terminism in capital markets, including portfolio turnover and equity holding periods by asset managers, whether practices in capital markets generate undue short-term pressure in the real economy.

Based on the EU taxonomy, the practical solutions for investment professionals to climate change mitigation

- Provide appropriate signals and more certainty
- Protect private investors and mitigate the risk of greenwashing
- Make it easier to raise capital for sustainability projects
- Address and avoid the market fragmentation and barriers to cross border capital flows
- Provide the basis for further policy action

---

[1] Europäische Investitionsbank, "Evaluierung des Europäischen Fonds für strategische Innovation," EIB 2021

The EU plans a historic investment of up to 2 trillion Euro in its economies from 2021. These will be provided from the EU budget (Multiannual Financial Framework (MFF)) and recovery funds (via Next Generation EU). Investments include infrastructure projects, i.e., smart cities.

The Taxonomy Regulation was published in the *Official Journal of the European Union* on 22 June 2020 and entered into force on 12 July 2020. Articles 10–15 of the Taxonomy Regulation lay down the main requirements for an economic activity to be considered as "substantially contributing" to these objectives:

- Climate change mitigation
- Climate Change adaptation
- Sustainable use of water and marine resources
- Transition to circular economy
- Pollution prevention and control
- Protection and/or restoration of biodiversity and ecosystems

All of this was planned and scheduled before the COVID-19 pandemic, the war in Ukraine, the economic setbacks of the recent past, and especially the high inflation. But obviously the challenges of the climate crisis do not go away because of current threats for the world economy. We still have to ask:

What is the central bank's contribution to ecological transformation? And to what extent will the knowledge gained from creating the taxonomy play a role in the ECB's bond and share purchases? What role does taxonomy play specifically for bond purchases?

With regard to quantitative easing (QE), a paper (Dafermos et al. 2020) argues that the ECB should abandon its position of market neutrality and must pursue a clearly climate-friendly strategy on all levels. The mandate is already being expanded, and central bank policy is also helping to stabilize state budgets—why not aim for the most important stabilization, namely, that of ecological balance? The scientists recommend paying particular attention to "green bonds," for which a description within the framework of clear taxonomic rules is of course important. Whether a "green bond" is really "green" and what that means can hardly be described without taxonomic clarity.

2 The Question of Market Neutrality

The paper mentioned above describes an essential fork in the road or an alternative in the ECB's strategy: *market neutrality and exclusive focus on monetary stability* or the *design of the economic framework for the ecological transformation in the financial sector*.

As we know, the primary objective of the Union's monetary policy is to maintain price stability. Without prejudice to that objective, the monetary's policy of the EU is to support the general economic policies in the Union with a view to contributing to the achievement of its objectives. These union objectives are laid down in Article

3(3) of the Treaty on European Union (TEU) that provides that the Union "shall work for the sustainable development of Europe based on balanced economic growth and price stability, a highly competitive social market economy, aiming at full employment and social progress, and a high level of protection and improvement of the quality of the environment."

I would like to argue here that taxonomy is important for both ways. Due to the importance of the taxonomy for institutional investors in particular but also for private investors, it can play a role for both strategies:

- For an approach in which the ECB's goals are interpreted in such a way that the focus is primarily on monetary stability, the taxonomy offers a better description of the products that can be described as "sustainable" and makes chains of effects visible around a new form of risk management to allow.
- For an approach in which the ECB is given a further mandate and its power to shape social and environmental conditions is emphasized, the taxonomy provides an overview of the characteristics of the appropriate instruments for such intervention. It can also be used to better assign asset classes to specific transformation strategies. The taxonomy has the task of describing real effects and making it understandable why some investments have an "impact" and others do not.

As a result, the risk assessment and risk management change with the definitions of the taxonomy. And the new description can be used market neutrally or market modeling.

In a press release dated 8 July 2021 ("ECB presents action plan to take climate protection aspects into account in its monetary policy strategy"), the important points are emphasized again, and the basic premises are made clear: "Although it is primarily the responsibility of governments and Parliaments to take action against climate change, but the ECB recognizes the need to include climate protection aspects in its monetary policy framework within its mandate. Climate change and the transition to a more sustainable economy affect the outlook for price stability as they affect macroeconomic indicators such as inflation, output, employment, interest rates, investment and productivity, financial stability and monetary policy transmission. In addition, climate change and the transition to a low-carbon economy have an impact on the value and risk profile of assets on the Eurosystem's balance sheet. This may lead to an undesirable concentration of climate-related financial risks."

Of particular interest is the Delegated Act supplementing Article 8 of the Taxonomy Regulation (published in the Official Journal on 10 December 2021 and applicable since January 2022).

3 Figures and Norms: Example Stress Test

The greater standardization in the description and naming of environmentally relevant activities and products means that, for example, stress tests such as the one recently carried out on climate change are professionalized and standardized and thus provide more solid figures. And without reliable figures, the implementation of standards will be very difficult. This 2022 climate change stress test was launched by the ECB to reassess risk profiles and better prepare banks for the financial and economic impact of the climate catastrophe. One bank did not fail the test, but there was a lot of critical feedback. "Euro area banks urgently need to step up their efforts to measure and manage climate risk," said ECB Banking Supervisor Andrea Enria, presenting the results of the ECB's first climate stress test.

In unfavorable scenarios, environmental losses for the industry are likely to add up to at least 70 billion euros. The sum relates to 41 of the 104 banks in the test. It reflects "only a fraction" of the actual climate-related risk for the industry, warned the supervisors. The Deputy Head of ECB Banking Supervision, Frank Elderson, emphasized: "We expect banks to act decisively and develop robust climate stress tests in the short to medium term." At this point, it becomes clear how and why the banks themselves need the language rules and descriptions of effects from the taxonomy.

The financial institutions directly supervised by the ECB had to calculate how well they are prepared for financial and economic shocks from climate risks: extreme heat, severe flooding, falling property prices, higher infrastructure costs, and drastically rising price for the emission of climate-damaging carbon dioxide.

This gives rise to many questions for day-to-day business: How do such scenarios affect real estate financing? How great is the risk that the green transition of the economy will cause problems for corporate customers and result in losses for banks? What is the time horizon for the transformation strategy for the system as a whole but also for individual players in the market? Depending on how quickly politicians initiate measures to slow down global warming, the risks will have a greater or lesser impact.

This was modeled in the aforementioned stress test in three scenarios over a 30-year period. Supervisors acknowledged that banks have made "some progress" in addressing climate risks since 2020. However, around 60% of the institutions now under scrutiny did not yet have a stress testing framework to model the climate risk for their business. Only 20% considered climate risks as a factor in lending.

The stress test also found that in the business with corporate customers of the institutes, almost two thirds of the income comes from greenhouse gas-intensive sectors. In a third part of the stress check, banks had to calculate losses resulting from extreme weather events such as heat waves and floods and under various transition scenarios.

4 Impact of Taxonomy

If we assume that the taxonomy also provides important foundations for the market-neutral approach to these stress tests, it is clear that the exchange of information and the merging of individual analyzes play a particularly important role. The taxonomy makes it possible to integrate the findings and provides an essential bridge between quantitative and qualitative surveys.[2]

This exchange could be improved if, on the one hand, the methods used to develop the taxonomy were more transparent and, on the other hand, databases and algorithms were made available with which one's own taxonomies could be prepared depending on the context of the study.

In any case, with or without technical support, the taxonomy is changing the market and the way market participants communicate with each other.

It requires implementation strategies in the various areas of the financial sector. For example, the German Banking Association has published a "Guide to the EU Taxonomy for Sustainable Investments—Six Questions and Answers for Credit Institutions" to enable institutions to easily meet their reporting obligations. Orientations and guidelines are conceivable for a wide range of areas, for fund houses, insurance companies, etc., which on the one hand facilitate the task of the ECB and on the other use findings and language regulations of the EU taxonomy.

This is summarized very well in the following quote: "The ECB has not yet defined the 'environmental sustainability' that it is going to integrate in its monetary policy. Indeed, it is probably not necessary for the ECB to do so. The EU legislator has already established an exhaustive list of environmental objectives for the purpose of determining the environmental sustainability of a given economic activity. It has done so in the piece of legislation to which this Conference panel is devoted: the Taxonomy Regulation."

Therefore, the same authors also come to the conclusion: "Thus, the Taxonomy Regulation is already of immediate use to the ECB and to the European System of Central Banks: by means of this Regulation, the fight against climate change (mitigation and adaptation), like the other environmental objectives mentioned above, is included in the EU's definition of environmental sustainability." The taxonomy thus stimulates a process of reflection on sustainability criteria and thus determines the framework in which the ECB moves with its sustainability policy.

References

Dafermos, Y., et al. (2020). "Decarbonising is easy. Beyound Market Neutrality in the ECB's corporate QE", New Economics Foundation 2020

ECB, ESCB Legal Conference 2020 https://www.ecb.europa.eu/pub/pdf/other/ecb.escblegalconferenceproceedings2020~4c11842967.en.pdf

Europäische Investitionsbank, "Evaluierung des Europäischen Fonds für strategische Innovation", EIB 2021

[2]More about this integration: György árhelyi, "EU Taxonomy and the monetary policy prism," in: ECB, ESCB Legal Conference 2020, p. 144ff

GPSR Compliance
The European Union's (EU) General Product Safety Regulation (GPSR) is a set of rules that requires consumer products to be safe and our obligations to ensure this.

If you have any concerns about our products, you can contact us on

ProductSafety@springernature.com

In case Publisher is established outside the EU, the EU authorized representative is:

Springer Nature Customer Service Center GmbH
Europaplatz 3
69115 Heidelberg, Germany

www.ingramcontent.com/pod-product-compliance
Ingram Content Group UK Ltd.
Pitfield, Milton Keynes, MK11 3LW, UK
UKHW020821290926
15470UKWH00003B/1304

* 9 7 8 3 0 3 1 2 4 4 7 7 3 *